Meet Me Backstage

Book 4 of the Arrowsmith High Series

MJ Ray

Copyright

♥

or locales or persons, living or dead, is entirely coincidental.

All publicly recognizable characters, settings, etc. are the property of their respective owners. The original characters and plot are the property of the author of this story. The author is in no way associated with the owners, creators or producers of any previously copyrighted material. No copyright infringement is intended.

Dedication

A strange one this, but this time I dedicate this book to myself. As someone that has suffered from anxiety at an early age it really was a personal journey for me, writing this book and if you do suffer from this affliction, I hope this book helps you.

Contents

Chapter One

Heidi

W hy is my brain wired this way? My heart is thumping so hard it feels like it's in the back of my throat.

Come on, Heidi, deep breath in through the nose... out through your mouth... slow exhale. Just like you've done a million times. You can get a handle on this.

Whether or not talking to myself is healthy, it strangely helps. A panic attack because a boy spoke a few words, is bad, even for me!

Oh god. Is he still talking?

I glance at Ethan, the guy sitting next to me, rambling about this science project. Science is not something I care about, at all. Leaving is all I care about right now. My fingers move as though they're on the strings of a guitar against the table; a calming technique of mine, memorising the actions and chords in my head.

It starts working and my heart rate goes back to a healthy speed just as I hear Ethan say, "So, what do you think? Should we meet up?"

We've been put into pairs - my worst nightmare. School is aware of my anxiety, but I didn't want any special consideration in class. That was my decision, but now, I'm kinda regretting it; now I'm paired with a boy... a good-looking one at that. He's on the rugby team, and has thick dark unruly brown hair. Yeah, he's cute. It's even worse when the cute ones try to talk to me. I just want to be left alone.

I clear my throat. "Sure, I guess we could meet in the library at lunch one day?" My voice doesn't sound like my own, but I'm still proud I'm able to speak.

He half-smirks to himself and shakes his head. "Sure, that's fine. Next week we'll organise a time for it."

The bell goes as I nod at him while keeping my eyes on my textbook. Eye contact is an impossibility. For me, looking at a boy is like trying to stare directly at the sun - don't do it or I'll implode.

I scramble to get my things together to get out as quickly as possible and get home.

Everyone else rushes out, eager to start their weekends. Murmurs about the party go around. There is a party tonight happening at a club nearby. It's a guy in our year, George; it's his birthday and his parents hired a room for the party. I'm sick of hearing about it, but I'm going with Harper and Sara and a few others. Crowds are fine, because I can blend in and stay hidden. It would come as a shock to half these people that I can't talk to them. They see what they want to see.

Grateful that I only live ten minutes' walk away from school, I step into the school courtyard and the sun hurts my eyes like I've been held underground all day. Rushing, I turn the corner towards the main exit and barrel into something... or someone. Crap, it's a someone. We collide, my bag dropping and the contents spilling on the floor. Seriously!

I bend to pick them up as fast as I can. My serious stationery addiction is obvious looking at the contents. Most girls own makeup and perfume...but me? It's highlighters, all types of nib pen, tape, glue, you name it with guitar picks thrown in there. The items in this bag are a window to my personality, and I'd prefer to keep it to myself. After picking up the last item, I look up to apologise and continue looking up and up. My blood runs cold. Please no. Not him, anyone but him. I'd recognise those legs anywhere.

My voice stops in my throat as I go to speak. It is him. Cooper. The Cooper that I've had a secret crush on for the last two years and avoided. I usually just gaze at him from a distance. This is not a distance. He's inches away. Cooper is Ed's twin. Ed is my friend's boyfriend and the nicest, most easy-going guy you could meet. Cooper is his twin brother and the polar opposite of all of that. He

3

is brooding and quiet – there's always something going on behind those eyes of his.

I only have one way to play it. Flirt, flick my hair and tell him how sorry I am while fluttering my eyelashes? But nooooo, instead I will be staring at the floor, saying nothing. Is there a word for the opposite of flirting? That's what I'm doing.

"When someone causes an accident, it's usual for them to apologise." He says in a level, bored tone. His voice is so deep. It should be, I guess. He's eighteen and technically an adult.

I keep my eyes on the floor, my heart hammering again, picking up where it left off. "I... I'm..." I stop and close my eyes for a second and take a deep breath.

Don't let this overtake you, Heid.

Just two words. "I'm sorry." I croak out.

He sighs and bends to help me. "Whatever."

He collects a couple of my books and hands them to me. His hand brushes mine as he hands them over and I snatch my hand away. What is wrong with me?

We both stand at the same time, and I fleetingly meet his eyes. He shakes his head and walks away in the opposite direction. My first communication with the boy I'm crushing on was an actual disaster, and he wasn't even nice. Although, I guess he *did* help me instead of walking away. I carry on towards the exit when I see Sara. She spots me and waits at the gates, smiling at me. We live next door to each other, so we walk home together if neither of us has an after school club or practice.

Sara eyes me. "Okay, what's the matter?"

I frown. "Why would anything be the matter?" I smooth my hair down. I feel dishevelled, but more because of interacting with Cooper than the crash.

"You're pale and sweaty. Let me guess... a guy tried to talk to you."

Oh, she has a way with words to make me feel pretty.

Sara knows about my fear of talking to boys. It is a true curse to be crippled with painful shyness.

I shake my head and roll my eyes. "Don't. You didn't see it. On two occasions in the last hour, I mortified myself."

She sighs. "Talk to me."

"Well let's see, there's Ethan in science..."

She interrupts. "Ooh, Ethan is fit. I've been trying to catch his eye for a while."

"Yeah, he's okay, I guess. Maybe that's why I couldn't look at him. So, he wanted to meet with me to go over a project and I couldn't even speak, nearly had a panic attack right there in the lesson."

"Oh, Heidi. What *are* we going to do with you?"

"I'm not even attracted to him, but he's not a girl, so I froze. Not that I can talk to girls that well, either."

"Yeah, but you're a tonne better with us girls. It's the male of the species that's the main of your problem."

I nod, "Oh, that's not it, it gets worse. Rushing to get out of school, I crashed right into Cooper, Ed's brother -

like, literally ran into him. Knocked his phone out of his hand and the stuff in my bag went everywhere. And he was mean, made me feel awful."

"Yeah, don't take that personally. I've never seen him crack a smile. How can twins be so different?"

She has no idea I've been crushing on him. He has the guts to be who he wants to be, a loner... different. I would love to have the guts to be myself. I don't have it in me - but he does, and he does it so well.

"They're so different. Harper loves him. She says he's a good person." They pretend not to get on, but that's all it is - pretend - she loves him like a brother.

"Yeah, well, it's different when you've grown up with someone since they were a baby. She doesn't see him that way. Plus, she's in love with his brother."

"I guess. Anyway, I'm gonna practice for half an hour when I get home, before I get ready - it'll calm me."

"Don't you ever get bored of playing that guitar?"

Is she crazy? I would do it all day long if I could. "God no, it calms me, keeps me level. I'd go insane if I couldn't play. Playing takes me to somewhere different, anywhere but the real world."

"Well, when you're a famous musician, guitar player, whatever, don't forget lil' ol' me who supported you on these walks to and from school."

I huff. "Oh yeah, I'm sure I'll be famous...you know, as long as I can sing in a pitch-black room, with no one watching me. That'll be fine. There's lots of demand for that, right?"

She chuckles, "Maybe somewhere, never give up hope."

I change the subject as it's something I can't see ever being a problem I can solve. "So, what time are you coming?"

She scrunches her nose, "Dunno. Not too early, maybe leave at eight thirty? Everybody will go around then. Should I come round to yours around seven and we can get ready together?"

I nod. "Yeah, that's fine. You still wearing that red dress?"

"Of course, I'm still in love with it. Lipsy never lets me down."

We chat about the party until we separate when we get to the bottom of my drive.

When I walk into the house, Mum calls out, "Heidi, is that you?"

I roll my eyes.

No Mum, it's Chris Hemsworth. He's come to take you away from all this and whisk you away to Australia.

I walk into the living room where she is sitting on the settee, working on her laptop.

I answer. "Yeah, it's me. Have you remembered I'm going to the party tonight?"

She nods. "Sure have. Don't forget me and your dad are going out, so you're sure you're coming home in a taxi with Sara?"

I nod. "Yeah, don't worry and I'll text you when I get home."

She frowns. "I don't like you going to these parties, but his parents arranged this one, didn't they?"

I nod and sigh. Why do my parents have to be so overprotective? "Yeah, it's supervised." I don't actually know if it's supervised, it's not like I've gone to him and asked if his parents will be there. Does she want me to get bullied? So, I fluff over the truth. She'll never find out.

She nods and narrows her eyes at me. "You alright?"

I sigh. She can read me like a book now. "Tough day. Nearly had one, but controlled it."

"That's brilliant, love, well done!"

"Yeah, I guess. I just wish it wasn't a thing. It's so embarrassing. People think I'm weird."

She frowns and puts her laptop to the side of her, standing to face me. "Honey, no one gets how hard it is for you to walk through those school doors some days. But you do it. Do you have any idea the strength that takes? You have an amazing strength because you push yourself and try to control it. You are amazing. And you will learn how to control this thing. You are doing all you can, you will see, you'll get a handle on it."

She annoys me sometimes with her protectiveness, but she gets me, and I love her for that. "Thanks. I want to learn to get a handle on it. I don't want to go through life with everybody thinking I'm a freak." I lean in and hug her. She understands because it runs in the family, it's something she suffered with at different times in her life. It makes it so much easier when there's someone on my side. My dad finds it harder to get his head around. He tries, but he struggles. My older sister doesn't see me much, she lives in Oxford where she goes to Uni, so we only see her on the holidays. She is fine, no anxiety other than the normal healthy amount - guess she got my dad's genes, but she's brilliant, she always has my back. She sees what Mum and Dad are like with me, too overprotective, and she always tries to reason with them, but she's never home, so she doesn't see the half of it.

Mum says my anxiety is my superpower. If only I agreed with her. She says it makes me aware of everyone and everything in my surroundings and gives me empathy. She's trying to make me feel better.

"The thing is, Heidi, you believe that you're the only one that feels this way. People have a lot going on in their heads that you don't know about, I promise you that. Give it time." She claps her hands together, ending the subject. "Now. What's the plan? What do you want for dinner?"

I shrug. "I'm gonna get in the shower and wash my hair. Anything will do."

"Chicken and rice? I've got some fried rice meal in the fridge?"

"Sure." I kiss her on the cheek and make my way upstairs.

Let's see what tonight's party brings, a night of my friends chatting to guys while I stare at the floor - ah, what fun!

Chapter Two

Cooper

I end the track and put down my drumsticks, the adrenaline rushing through my body, as it always does when I'm playing.

Jay jumps onto the stage. "Bro, that was amazing. Your drumming has seriously gone up a level," he says, grinning.

I give him a chin lift. "Thanks dude, it's coming together." With all the practicing I've been doing, it should be.

"Yeah, we just need a bloody singer, then we're laughing."

I shrug. "You do fine."

He shakes his head. "I'm not a singer, you know that. I'm a bass player. Singing isn't my thing. Your songs are brilliant, man. They need to be sung by someone that can bring the house down, plus the songs we've written, they would sound awesome with a female lead."

He's right, we need a singer, but hey, can't have everything. Baby steps. It will be good when it all comes together. Maybe a little more practice, then we can ask around for a singer. We need to get it together first.

I dismount from my stool and glance around the place. Everyone is doing their own thing, and I smile to myself, grateful again that I can come here - even if Edward is the only one that knows I come here.

It started as a pool hall, somewhere to meet, then as people heard how cool it was, it morphed into a place where people come for all sorts of things. You name it - you can do it here. The owner, Derek, is so cool. A self-made millionaire that grew up around here. When he was a teenager, there wasn't anywhere for kids to hang out. He bought this place so that kids our age would have somewhere to go. He hires someone to manage it but shows up from time to time. We all love him. He created a place where us misfits could come and be ourselves and we're grateful for that. In a world where it's hard to express yourself, if you don't play sports, be the most popular kid in your year, you're not worth anything, right? It's the opposite here. You can be yourself, and that's saying something. The places you can just be yourself are limited when you're eighteen.

Two guys I hang with are playing cards in the corner. I check the time, ten to ten; hmmm, another hour on the drums or play cards with those guys. The drums win out... another hour, then I'll take off. The more practice I get, the better. I get such a buzz from playing. If I'm not writing songs somewhere, I'm playing here or at school.

My phone rings, 'Harper Calling'. I frown. Why is Harper calling me?

I press answer. "Hey, Harper."

"Oh Cooper, thank God! Where are you?"

I hear the panic in her voice. "What's wrong?"

"It's just - I need your help. It's Heidi."

Who the hell is Heidi?

"Who is Heidi?" I ask her, what the hell is going on?

Harper sighs as though I'm hard work, "Cooper, she's one of my best friends!"

Then it dawns on me. She's the clumsy one that barged into me earlier and didn't say sorry. What was her deal? She wouldn't even make eye contact with me. That girl has issues.

"What about her?" I ask.

"There's something wrong with her. I've never seen her like this. I think... she could be drunk." Her voice goes into a whisper at the end.

"Wait. You drink at these parties?" I mean, they're sixteen and they get it from somewhere. Harper and her friends drinking, though? I can't see it.

"What! No, of course not. Someone must have spiked her drink or something. I - she's acting weird, she's acting kind of drunk."

My stomach churns at the thought of someone doing that to one of Harper's friends. Would anyone stoop that low? "Are you sure?"

"Yeah, I'm sure it's alcohol. She's acting giddy and, well, that's not Heidi. She's not the giddy type."

"You can say that again." I can't help myself.

"Hey! You don't know her. I never thought you would judge someone without knowing them."

She's right. I was out of order. "Ok, sorry, so what do you want me to do?"

"Well, her parents are out. I don't want to phone them because they'll go crazy, they're mad protective, and Edward is watching Manchester Giants tonight with Liam, so he's out. It's a lot to ask and I'm so sorry, but could you pick us up? I don't know who else to ask without us getting in tonnes of trouble." Harper pleads.

"Are you sure this isn't self-inflicted? Maybe she wanted to let loose." She sure needed to loosen up.

"You don't know Heidi, but trust me, she would never drink intentionally." Her voice turns into a whisper. "I think someone in here did it. Please, Coop." She's pleading now. Like I can say no.

I sigh. Of course I'm not going to leave her stranded. "Give me the address." She rattles off an address. "I'll be there in twenty minutes."

"Thank you, thank you, thank you." Her voice breaks. I end the call and grab my coat and my keys and say bye to the guys.

I close the car door with a slam, trying to keep my cool but failing miserably. What sicko would do that to a sixteen-year-old girl? Either a girl, jealous of her, or a guy trying to get somewhere with her. She is gorgeous, though. Weird, but gorgeous. Her wavy bobbed hair makes me want to run my hands through it and those tortoise-shell glasses really suit her. She's not exactly approachable, which makes me think some guy could have wanted to make her more approachable. I clench my fists and unclench them, trying to keep my temper in check as I walk up the path.

I text Harper that I've arrived and wait for her to come out. After a couple of seconds, the door to the club swings open and Harper's terrified face meets me. "Thank God, Coop - I owe you one for this. You'll need to help me. She's swaying around and losing her balance, and she might look like she weighs nothing but, believe me, she does not. I need your help."

I sigh and stare at the floor. How the hell did I get landed with this? Harper isn't my girlfriend, she's my brother's, he should be here dealing with this. It's not even her that needs the help, it's her friend. But who am I kidding? Harper's like a little sister to me, but even if she was a stranger, I wouldn't see a girl in trouble, especially because of what some idiot did to her.

I step inside the clubroom and follow Harper into a large darkened room with lights flashing from the DJ stand. Kids from school are milling around being loud and annoying, the opposite of a situation I'd usually like to be involved in. You couldn't drag me here.

I follow her to another room - a small private bar at the other end of the party room. My heart lurches as I see Heidi slumped on a bench with her head down.

Okay, Coop, keep calm.

Harper squats down to her and puts her hands on her knees. "Hey, Heidi, time to go. Our lift is here."

She raises her head, and her zoned-out eyes meet mine. Something shoots through me as though someone has punched me. I've never seen her eyes before. They're an unusual honey colour, sort of a light brown with bright gold flecks, making them almost transparent - seriously cool. Although right now, they appear dead; she's out of it.

She smiles at me, and it hits me again how pretty she is. "Ed, I knew you'd come. Harper loves you." She narrows her eyes at me again and realises that I'm not my twin and her eyes widen. "Wait, you're not Edward, you're his mean brother, Cooper."

She turns to Harper. "What is Cooper doing here? He hates me." She leans in and whispers, "I wish he didn't, though. He's way hotter than Edward." She puffs out air and fans her face and I bite back a grin. Not sure why she thinks I hate her, I've never even had cause to speak to her.

Harper flashes me a glance. She doesn't know whether to laugh or cry - she turns back to Heidi, "I couldn't get hold of Ed and Cooper stepped up, so be nice or he'll leave us. K?" She's talking to her as though she's a baby. Remorse flashes in Heidi's eyes and she leans into Harper, whispering loudly, "It's okay, I don't really think he's mean, I think he so gorgeous I can't even look at him."

Now I full out laugh. She will die inside tomorrow. Still, kinda like that I have an effect on the girl.

Harper's attention turns to me, grinning. "Well, you gonna help me or not? And please pretend you didn't hear that." She stands and grabs Heidi's hand, "Come on, rock chick, time to get you home."

"Why do you call her rock chick?" I ask.

She shakes her head. "Sorry, personal joke."

Hmmm, this girl is getting more and more interesting.

Heidi slowly tries to stand on Bambi legs, then plops back down. Yeah, no way she can walk. Can I carry her? She's slim but tall, it's not gonna be easy. Plus, everyone at the party will see me carry her out. She will be the talk of the school on Monday. If I can support her weight and she can walk, it will be so much better and save her the embarrassment.

I bend and get hold of her arm, throwing it around my shoulder, and slide my arm around her waist. "Okay, work with me, try to stand and I'll support your weight." I can't help but notice how she smells of apple blossom. What is going on with me and my reactions to her? I'm noticing her scent – who does that?

17

She stands and I take most of her weight as we walk. "Don't tell, but I like you the best." She mumbles as she slides her hand around my waist, grabbing firmly at my t-shirt there. I've gotta say, I don't hate the feeling.

"Glad to hear it. Concentrate on where your feet are going."

"That's why I can't look at you," she says, sadly.

"Why wouldn't you be able to look at me?" Trying to talk and get her out isn't easy, but I want to know why she has such a reaction to me.

"You're scary and too hot to talk to me." Her words are slurring at this point.

"I look exactly like Ed, and you're friends with him."

She shakes her head, lolling it from side to side. "Oh no, you're nothing like Ed."

I smile to myself. She's right - we're identical in appearance, but that's where the similarity ends. He's all 'ray of sunshine' and I'm a storm cloud. Even Mum says it.

"No, I'm not, you're right. Come on. We're nearly outside." Harper has hold of her on the other side. People are watching. It's obvious she's hammered, so I guess hiding it didn't work too well.

She puts even more of her body weight on me, leaning into me further. "Do you want to kiss me?"

I can't hold back my chuckle. "I'm good, thanks. Maybe another time." She will be mortified in the morning and through no fault of her own. I'm gonna ask around about this. It's one thing choosing to drink at these parties, but it's a whole different matter getting that decision taken away from you.

We get to the car, and I lift her in. "You're so strong."

These compliments could go to a guy's head.

Harper rolls her eyes. "Yes, Heidi, he's so strong, now don't go to sleep and don't throw up." She glances at me. "This is just booze, right?"

I assess Heidi. She just seems drunk. I nod. "Yeah, I'm pretty sure. Any idea who did it?"

She shakes her head, "No, no way, not a clue. She had a can of coke when we went to the bathroom. Maybe someone put it in her drink then?"

I frown. "You didn't take your drinks with you?"

"Well, no, it was the toilet, and we trusted the guys that were there. There was a windowsill outside the bathroom. We left it on there."

How could they be so stupid? I shake my head. "Seriously?"

She frowns. "Now is not the time for a lecture. Can we go home? This night has been a disaster."

"I want to play." Heidi mutters.

What? Play what?

Harper says, "She plays guitar."

I *knew* this girl was interesting.

"Is that what the 'rock chick' comment was about?"

"Yeah, it's a joke because she is the opposite of a rock chick, but she plays rock music when she plays."

I stiffen. "Does she play at school?"

She shrugs. "Yeah, why?"

I shake my head. "No reason."

Could she have been the one playing that day? I tried to question the music teacher about the identity of the guitar player without seeming too keen, but the music lover in me needs to find out. Whoever was playing is talented. Maybe I'll make a few more enquiries on Monday. I take in her glasses, her outfit, all of her. She doesn't seem like the secret guitar player, but what does an amazing guitar player look like? There are no rules. I would be something else if it was her...

I sigh and get in the car. I can't believe they left their drinks unattended. Who does that at a party?

We pull up to Heidi's house. There are no lights on – her parents are still out which is a relief. Heidi's head slumps down, almost touching her knees. She is struggling to stay awake, or maybe she's already lost that battle. "Heidi, do you have a key?" I ask.

She mumbles something about her bag, so Harper fumbles through it and retrieves the key. "Her parents are out tonight. She was supposed to come home with Sara and message them when she was home. I'll text them from her phone when I get her settled. If they find out about this, they'll never let her out again. They're so overprotective of her because of her.... well, it doesn't matter, but it's best they don't know. Sara wanted to stay at the party once she knew you were coming. She's getting a lift with her other friend's dad."

"You need to tell her parents, Harp. This is serious."

She sighs. "I'll talk to Heidi about it tomorrow when she's awake."

I nod and get out of the car, walking round to the back where Heidi is slumped. Harper gets out too. I nod towards the door. "You go open the door and I'll carry her inside."

I bend to talk to Heidi. "I'm gonna carry you. Can you put your arms around my neck?"

She lifts her head, and her eyes meet mine. There are tears in them. "I don't like this feeling."

Anger washes through me again. How could someone do this to her? This shouldn't have happened.

"I know, honey, I'm sorry that this happened to you, but you'll be right as rain tomorrow. Well, maybe you'll be feeling a little ill, but you'll feel more like yourself."

She shakes her head, and a tear rolls down. "Someone like you would never look at someone like me."

My gut twists to hear her say that. She has such a low opinion of herself.

"Why do you say that? Why wouldn't I look at you?"

She shakes her head. "You just wouldn't. I'm so sorry you've had to come."

"Don't apologise. None of this is your fault. And by the way, if you are who I think you are, you're bloody amazing."

Those honey eyes stare at me, and she gives me a small smile.

I lean even closer to her, "Put your arms around my neck. I've got you."

She whispers, "You've got me." And then she does as I ask, as I slide my arms under her legs and lift her from the car, adjusting her so that I have hold of her firmly. I straighten and make my way down her path.

She's so vulnerable. I have the sudden urge to take care of her, a girl I don't even know.

I'm almost at the front door when I hear, "What the hell are you doing to my daughter?"

Oh crap. Terrible timing.

I turn around and a man and woman are stalking towards us. The woman looks Korean, and the man is tall with greying hair. They're obviously Heidi's parents. Well, isn't this perfect timing? My night was going so well until I answered my phone. Why do I own a mobile phone... but then, I look at Heidi, in my arms, her head resting on my chest, her glasses crooked. Helpless. No, I'm glad I answered the phone, whatever happens next.

Chapter Three

Cooper

"Your daughter isn't well, so I'm seeing her home." They'll never believe me, even I can see this doesn't look good and I know it's innocent.

"Put her down. Put her down right now!" they shout. "What the hell have you done to her?"

Her dad is furious but I'm sure they don't want me to put her down in the middle of their driveway. There's no way her legs will support her. My arms are going to drop off if I don't put her somewhere soon. I ignore him and walk towards the house where Harper has gone inside. Yeah, cheers Harper.

I step inside as I hear her dad's voice bellowing. "How dare you go inside our home!"

I sigh and walk inside, ignoring the ogre behind me. I see the living room and carefully place her on the couch. She curls away from me, her face in a cushion, and starts to snore lightly. I can't help but smile to myself. She hasn't got a care in the world right now. Harper is flustered and grabs a throw to cover her. She speaks to Heidi's parents. "Mr and Mrs Garrett - it's not what it looks like."

Her Mum speaks in an uppity tone. "Well, it doesn't look too good, does it? Would one of you want to tell me what has happened to my daughter tonight?"

Harper sighs, "I'm not sure what happened. We're guessing that she had alcohol, that someone maybe spiked her drink."

Her mum gasps and goes to sit on the couch with a snoring Heidi.

"You think it's alcohol? How sure are you? Do we need to take her to hospital?" Her dad asks Harper, ignoring that I'm standing there.

I turn to him, "She was acting drunk, giddy, happy, she's fine, she'll sleep it off."

He steps into me and grabs my jacket, leaning into me. "You need to get out of here now before I do something to a teenager that'll end with me getting arrested. This isn't the last you'll hear of this. I'll be speaking to your parents, to school and to the police. You will regret ever messing with my daughter."

I preferred it when he was ignoring me.

Harper tries to speak, "Mr Garrett..."

But he carries on, he's on a roll. "And I don't want to speak to you either, young lady. You both better leave right now."

Well, this is a disaster.

I turn to Harper, knowing nothing can be resolved right now. "Come on, Harp, we better go."

There is silence as we leave and the door slams behind us. She cringes.

Once we're back on the road, she turns to me. "What a mess, I'm so sorry I got you caught in it."

I sigh, "Yeah, not one of my best nights. She'll put the record straight, right? When she wakes tomorrow?"

I don't want her dad on my warpath.

She nods, "Yes, of course she will. We will sort it out. I feel so awful, you doing this good deed for me and getting man handled by her dad."

"I get it, what dad wouldn't do that if he thought it was me that spiked her? Heidi will clear it up I'm sure, don't worry."

Let's hope she remembers....

I wake around ten and groan as last night comes flooding back to me. Crap, I suppose I better go tell Mum and Dad to expect a phone call. Unless she's already told them what happened, of course, but my guess is she'll still be sleeping. She was so innocent and vulnerable lying there on the couch. My blood boils. I need to find out who did this to her. Not just to clear my name but because they need to pay for doing that to an innocent girl.

I lie in my comfortable bed cocooned in my duvet, trying to force myself to get up. God, her eyes. Wow, I've never seen anything like them. She's so beautiful, but I shouldn't be thinking that right now, or ever. I need to sort this mess out. No wonder Harper dreaded phoning Heidi's parents, they are scary. Poor Heidi - they'd be hard to live with. She was so cute last night, and that invitation for a kiss was so tempting. Wouldn't mind kissing those lips of hers when she's sober though. Trouble is, when she's sober, she can't even meet my eye. Maybe that's why, maybe she's crushing on me. I like that. That, I can work with.

As I'm putting on my shorts, I hear Mum shout. "Cooper, can you come here for a minute?"

My stomach sinks. Time to face it.

I take my time going downstairs, Mum and Dad are both sitting on the couch in the living room.

I lean on the wall, "What's up?"

"Do you want to tell us something?" Mum bites her lip.

She doesn't believe I would spike some girl's drink, does she?

"Is this about last night?" My voice is rough from waking.

"I'd say so, I've just got off the phone from a furious and unpleasant man, accusing you of awful things," my dad says, "Tell me it's not true, son."

I open my mouth to speak and he raises his hand and carries on talking. "You wouldn't spike some girl's drink, we know that, but did you get this girl drunk?"

I shake my head, unbelievable. "Can't believe you'd think that. No, I didn't. She's sixteen. I wasn't even at that party."

Mum sighs, "You rarely even go to those parties. Why were you there?"

My dad speaks up. "Let him tell us what happened." They both stare at me, waiting for my side of the story.

"Why don't you ask Harper?"

Mum frowns. "Because we're asking you – why would we ask Harper?"

I snort, "I see Heidi's dad hasn't given you the full story."

I don't want to replay it all, but I don't have a choice. I explain what happened and Mum is relieved but Dad gets angrier and angrier as the tale goes on.

I finish, "So you can check with Harper when she's here later."

Dad shakes his head, "No need for that. You're telling me you went out to help a girl in trouble and you are getting punished for it?"

I shrug, "When you put it like that, yeah. He said he wanted to speak to you, school and the police, that I'd regret messing with his daughter. I'd hoped that Heidi was going to put him straight, but maybe she doesn't remember anything, she was out of it, or maybe she's still asleep."

Dad stands. "Right, that's it, get dressed. We're going there now and straightening this out."

"Is that a good idea, Brian?" Mum asks him, and I can tell he's on the brink of losing it.

"We're getting this sorted out once and for all. He's talking about going to the police, for God's sake, there's no way I'm letting this go on any longer. He's going to drag our son's name through the dirt when he should be thanking him."

I need to ask. "Did he say how Heidi was?"

"No, but we're going to find out. Get dressed, we're going now."

When my dad gets something in his head, there's no stopping him. I traipse back upstairs to get dressed. I don't want to go;; this might make things worse, but if we do get it sorted today then I won't be getting in trouble for something I didn't do.

And you want to see her to check she's okay, because you can't forget those eyes.

I shake my head to rid that thought.

We knock on the door and Shrek from last night answers with a scowl. His eyes narrow as he sees me. "I thought I said I didn't want to see your face again?"

Dad speaks before I have a chance. "We've come for a discussion about last night if that's okay. I think a few facts got mixed up."

"It seems straightforward to me." His body is covering the door frame, the signal clear: keep out.

I lean in to Dad. "Let's go."

If I know Dad, he will be fighting an internal battle between agreeing with me and steam coming out of his ears. Heidi's mum appears at the door behind Shrek. "Darren, don't you think we should at least hear them out? Especially after what Heidi told us."

I sigh and close my eyes. Thank God, Heidi has put them straight.

He turns to his wife. "What has she told us? Nothing, she can't remember a thing because of this idiot here."

My dad bristles and I can sense this getting out of hand, I need to speak. "All I did was bring Heidi home because of the state she was in, I wasn't even at the party."

He narrows his eyes at me, "You expect me to believe that?"

I hear a small voice coming from inside the house. "Dad, let them in, *please*, he can tell me what happened - I can't get through to Harper."

Jeez, thanks, Harper.

He sighs, "Fine, I wouldn't mind knowing either."

He steps back so we can go in, his eyes narrowed and fixated on me. We follow him into the living room where I see her. She's in the same spot I placed her last night.

Something rushes through me. What effect is she having on me? The urge to go over and put my arms around her is strong. She is so vulnerable sat there in her pyjamas, seeming a little worse for wear and so friggin' cute. Her face is make-up free, and she's swaddled in a throw. Her hair could have been plugged into electricity, it's so messy. Sympathy washes over me. None of this is her fault, some idiot did this to her - trouble is, her dad believes I'm that idiot and I need to convince him otherwise. He definitely does not go by the rule of innocent until proven guilty.

Her eyes widen when she sees me and she glances at her cup of tea. I see her inhale deeply. She probably wants to be sick.

"Are you alright?" I ask, gently.

She nods at her cup of tea as though her brew asked the question. "Yeah, I guess, events are still blurred...what happened?" Her voice is so quiet and shaky, I hardly hear it.

"I got a call from Harper last night, she said you needed help and asked me to come and get you both, she thought someone spiked your drink at the party. You were out of it when I got there, but I think you were just drunk. She says you both left your drink on a windowsill when you went to the toilet and she's presuming it happened there, but she's guessing."

Her mum gasps, and I turn to speak to her. "Harper will tell you this is true."

I turn back to Heidi, her head still down. Why won't she look at me? And why is it bothering me so much that she won't? She doesn't believe her dad, does she? Surely she remembers I wasn't even at the bloody party.

I sigh and shake my head. "Anyway, speak to Harper, she's probably still in bed. I'll knock on when I get home and get her to ring you as soon as possible."

Her eyes meet mine and pain shoots through me as that's all I see in hers. Pain and anguish. This girl is terrified. "I hardly remember any of the night. Did I do or say anything?"

I shake my head. She doesn't need to be told about wanting me to kiss her. She would crumble. "Nothing you need to worry about. I'm sorry this happened to you."

It's as though it's only me and her, and I forget that there is a man in the room that wants to kill me. I glance over to find him glaring at me, his jaw flexing, but he keeps silent, which is something.

I need to get out of here. Heidi knows what happened now and Harper will fill her in with the rest. She doesn't remember saying those things to me. If Harper is feeling charitable, she might not tell her. Who am I kidding? She can't resist a gossip, she will totally tell her, so this is probably the last time she'll talk to me.

Dad and I turn to leave, and I glance at Heidi, who has raised her head to watch me leave. Her honey eyes meet mine and something shoots through me I don't recognise. I give her a sad smile.

Her mum walks toward me. I tower above her she is so short. She grabs my arm. "Thank you... for taking care of her."

I nod. I'd say, 'you're welcome', but this is not fun, so they're not welcome, not at all. In fact, it's put me off helping anyone ever again.

But how can I say that when she's sat there vulnerable in her pyjamas not having a clue what happened to her? Her insides must be in knots, besides being hungover. No, I don't regret helping her, no matter what the consequences.

Chapter Four

Heidi

I inhale deeply as I step out of the front door. Fear fills me because I'm one step closer to school. I don't want to go to school for so many reasons today. One, my anxiety is through the roof. I had a massive panic attack on Saturday, worse than I've had in a long time. Mum even phoned the therapist but when she explained what had happened, the doctor said that alcohol will enhance the attack and make it more intense. No more drinking for me, ever. Not that I had a choice this time. Alcohol can aggravate anxiety and it certainly did with me. Dad insisted we go to A&E to have a blood test, to check it wasn't drugs or anything more sinister. The hospital staff were happy to do it when they heard what happened, especially as whatever it was, was escalating my panic attack. Four hours later, the blood test confirmed it was alcohol in my system. We phoned the police, but they said they couldn't do much without proof. Dad insisted on talking to George's dad - he wouldn't listen to me - so now everyone knows, and I have to face them today. George will tell the entire school.

Then there's wondering, who would do that to me? I've never been mean to anyone, why did I deserve that? The power that I should have, being in control of myself, has been stripped away from me. No one should have that power taken away from them. It's going to be someone at school that did it so I will suspect everyone today. The thought terrifies me that they could have done it for a sinister reason, even though it was probably so they'd get a laugh out of it. But Harper's drink wasn't spiked. She was fine. Someone could be watching me at school and I wouldn't know. Maybe that's my mind working overtime, but I didn't make up the fact that someone spiked me. It was probably someone from my school that did it and they'll know and I don't. I hate that.

Then there's him.

Harper told me what I said to him. I never want to face him, ever again. I still can't believe those words came out of my mouth. 'Do you want to kiss me?'

I groan. Even though I have no memory of it, my imagination can conjure it up perfectly... and his reaction. Although, Harper said he was sweet about it. What was it she said he said? 'I'm good thanks, maybe some other time.'

I wish. But at least he was a gentleman.

I go over to Sara's house, sympathy written all over her face as she answers the door. I texted her yesterday and she came over so that I could fill her in.

"Hey, how are you doing?"

I shrug, "I might throw up, for so many reasons, pick one."

We start the short journey to school. "I can't believe it. I still can't believe that one of our friends would do that."

I give a half-laugh, "Thing is though, Sara, we're told at school, in magazines, at home, never ever leave your drink, and Harper and I did exactly that—I'm so stupid. You always assume that's in a nightclub or something, not at a friend's birthday party. But we didn't recognise everyone there, did we?"

She shakes her head, "I saw a couple there that I didn't recognise, maybe they were friends of George's from cricket; he plays, right?"

I shrug, "I'm not sure."

"Have your parents told George's parents?"

I nod, "Yeah, I'm dreading seeing George. They were concerned blah, blah, but what can they do? George will have told half the school. I didn't want them to say anything. They're making things worse for me."

Sara sighs, "Yeah, I think they may have forgotten what it's like to be a teenager. They should have left it alone."

"Part of me gets it, I mean, we were stupid for leaving our drink – it could have been spiked with something more serious. Whoever did it probably wanted to have fun, laughing at someone's expense, but it could have a different reason." I shouldn't let my mind go there, but I can't help it. We won't ever find out.

"Yeah, it's scary as hell though, I will be more careful in future."

"I'm so sorry I left you at the party." I wince at her.

She waves it away, "Don't worry. Harper told me you were going, so I arranged a lift home with Dora's dad, it was fine. All was good, and it wasn't your fault. Have you heard from Cooper?"

I groan and my heart rate increases. "No, not since Saturday and I never want to see him ever again - well, after I apologise."

The thought of apologising to him and thanking him makes bile rise in my throat, but it's got to be done. I owe him big time. He does something good for someone he doesn't know and my dad phones his parents as though he is a criminal, for God's sake. Dad still isn't convinced he was being a 'knight in shining armour'. The guy came, got me to his car - where I could have thrown up, for all he knew - then carried me into the house while getting abused by my dad. He *was* my bloody knight in shining armour. I'll never forget it. Some guys can be nice. It had to be him, though, the guy I crush on. The guy I've liked for years. It's made me like him even more.

"It'll be fine, stop worrying. How's the anxiety?"

"Through the roof. I don't know how I'm gonna get through today, I want to be sick. I've done my Calm App.

Just got to remember to breathe, keep my head down and get through today. I need to apologise to him as soon as we get to school and then I don't need to see him again or worry about it all day. Once it's done, I can forget about it."

I can picture the awkward scene in my head now. Me blundering through an apology while Cooper wants to run screaming away from me. Ah well. Can't be any worse than the picture in my head...can it?

When we get to school, the yard is full. Harper is standing with Edward and a couple of girls from the bus. I go over; if they're there, it means that Cooper has arrived too as he gets the bus with them so he doesn't have to worry where to park his car.

They see me approach and I fix my eyes on Harper and nowhere else. Besides, seeing Edward makes me think of Cooper. They are identical twins, even if they are different in every other way.

"Heidi, how are you?" Riley, a girl from the bus asks - she's heard the news.

I give her a small smile. "I'm fine, thanks."

"It's disgusting what happened. How could someone do that?"

"Yeah, thanks, Riley." This is what it's going to be like all day. Everyone is going to be talking, the school grapevine makes things spread quicker than Snapchat. I'm probably on Snapchat somewhere falling all over the place. Great.

Well, might as well get it over with, I turn to Edward, "Is your brother around?"

"Yeah, he's gone over to the music block for something. You can get him there before the bell goes if you hurry."

I nod and turn to Sara. "See you later?"

She touches my arm. "It'll be fine, you'll feel better once it's done."

I nod.

I make my way over to the music block with shaky legs. Ironically, the music block is the one place I go to relax, but right now it's having the opposite effect.

The music block is unlocked but I don't see him, so I make my way inside. I can picture him hiding under a table somewhere in case I go searching for him. I bet he wants to avoid me like the plague. As I step into the corridor, I stop in my tracks as I see him reading a notebook, walking towards me.

I take a deep breath, "Hi." I clear my throat; my voice sounds croaky.

His head snaps up. He is so good looking. Those dark eyes stare straight at me. He has a perfectly straight nose. I mean, who notices noses for god's sake, but his is *perfect*! It's strange that I don't find Edward attractive - I mean, he has the same nose and eyes, but this guy, who is identical, I find attractive. He has a darker edge than

Edward. Maybe that's what I'm attracted to. Is it worrying that I'm attracted to someone with a dark edge? Probably.

"Heidi. How are you?" his voice is so deep.

"Um, mortified, thanks for asking."

He smirks. "So, Harper filled you in?"

I nod and try to meet his eyes, but they are going anywhere but to his face. The blood rushes straight to my cheeks.

"Don't worry about it." His voice is soft.

"I'm sorry you got grief off my dad." My bloody dad, I could kill him after this weekend. He's still adamant that Cooper has something to do with the state I was in. He is so stubborn and doesn't want to admit that he was wrong.

"Has he calmed down?"

I shrug, "A little. He is going to phone the school, he promised not about you though," Harper confirmed what happened, "but he's insisting that school should be informed."

He nods, "I don't blame him. You're lucky you had your friend taking care of you."

"Yeah, and you. I'm lucky I had you to help me too. I hate that I don't remember anything."

He tilts his head but doesn't say anything, I know he's watching me, so I meet his eyes finally. "What?"

"Do you play the guitar?"

My eyes almost pop out of my head and roll down the corridor. How the hell does he know? Did I tell him on

Friday night? "Er, um..." crap, what can I say? "A little," I mumble.

"Do you play in here?" He motions around the music block.

I nod but say nothing, please let us be done with this conversation.

He nods. "I heard someone after school one night a couple of weeks ago...Sweet Child O'mine, was that you?"

Oh god, he heard me. "Sometimes I practice here if Mr Ball lets me."

"So, it *was* you," he probes.

I meet his eyes again, "Yeah," I whisper.

"You're good."

I know I'm blushing, mortified that he heard me. "Thanks."

"No, I mean like *good* good. Where did you learn to play like that?"

I relax my shoulders. Music. Music I can talk about.

"When I was around eleven, I heard someone play, so I asked and asked for one for Christmas. Mum relented and talked my dad around, so I got one and self-taught for a couple of years with YouTube videos. When they saw it wasn't a passing phase, they signed me up for actual lessons."

"That is so cool. I play the drums, I wish my parents would see how serious I am about it, but whatever... it is what it is. What about you, do you play anywhere?"

My eyes widen, "God no, I could never..."

He takes a step towards me "You should. I might be able to help you with that."

I shake my head. "No thanks. I've got to go."

Before he can say anything else, I run out of the building. My heart is hammering through my chest. Why did words just blurt out of my mouth and pour out like lava all over the floor? God, anytime I talk about music I forget where I am. I hate this. I've opened up to the guy I never wanted to talk to again. Why did I have to mention it on Friday when I was drunk, for god's sake? Why did Friday night have to happen at all? I didn't want anyone to find out about playing the guitar - that's my thing–the thing that keeps me sane, reduces my stress, that and singing. I can lose myself, forget my anxiety and go off into another world. The last thing I want is someone asking questions. It seems I'm chatty when I'm drunk. Yet another reason I'm never ever drinking alcohol.

The bell goes and I rush to class. So, if he knows about me playing there's only one thing I can do: avoid him at all costs.

Chapter Five

♥

Heidi

"The school concert will take place in a month. Think of it as a talent show. It gives a chance for parents to see what the students get up to - how talented their children can be when they're behaving themselves and of course to show them that music teachers are brilliantly inspiring. The sign-up sheet is on the wall for anyone wanting to take part, and practice will start next week."

The music teacher stares at me. He can think again if he thinks I'm signing up for it. I'm sick of him asking me - doesn't he get it? I can't perform in front of people.

Sure, sir, I'll do it when Amazon goes out of business!

The bell goes off to signify the end of the lesson. Music is my favourite, but my stomach is in knots because I'm sure that the teacher is going to ask me to be part of the show.

We gather our things and start to leave. I nearly escape, nearly get to the door, when I hear, "Heidi, can I have a word for a second?"

My shoulders droop, the expectation of what is coming weighing heavily because while I can't perform, I can't say no to people. One day I will grow a backbone, but today is not that day.

I hang back until everyone leaves.

"Heidi, I want you to help in the concert," he says.

I shake my head, "I don't really want to."

He holds his hands up in surrender, "I know, I know. You don't want to perform, but you are so talented with anything to do with music, and we could use your expertise. You don't have to do anything you don't want to. What do you say?"

I guess it wouldn't hurt to be involved, might be what I need to push myself out of my comfort zone, especially if I'll be behind the scenes. It's not like I'm getting a choice anyway.

I nod. "Sure, I guess I could do that."

His eyes light up, "Brilliant. And about your song writing... I've heard you sing a couple of them." I nod and glance at the door. Please let me leave. "We have a talented writer in the sixth form. If I can get them to agree, you two could work together and come up with a couple of songs for the show."

"I prefer to work alone, sir."

He sighs, "And I get that, but if this is something you want to pursue, maybe you should try to work with others. If we don't feel fear about something, do we really care about it at all?"

He's right. I do need to push myself. Otherwise, why am I bothering? But it's so hard. He has no idea how hard.

I nod, "Okay, sir, I'll try."

He grins. "Great, I can't ask for more than that. I have your best interests at heart, Heidi. There will be a message going on 'Show My Homework' inviting us to a meeting at lunch and after that it will be after school on Wednesdays if you can make it."

I nod, "I can do that."

Leaving the classroom, I have butterflies in my stomach: two different species of butterflies, one of excitement and one of fear. They may have a fight at some point, we will see who wins. I guess that's up to me.

Dread fills me as I stand outside of the music room clutching onto my lunch as though it's Captain America's shield. Who is in there? The last thing I want is my lunch right now!

With a deep breath and my calming techniques in place, I step inside. Then my world gets fuzzy. Those eyes. They are the first and only thing I see as the room starts to spin. He can't be here. The guy I've been avoiding, running away from, the guy who I asked to kiss me. My heart beats so hard and things get hazy. I try to inhale deeply, but no, it's not going to happen, I'm not going to calm down this time - my calming techniques go to hell. I turn around to leave so no one sees me, but it's too late – the room blurs as I away. A chair scrapes in the distance as arms wrap around me, then the blurry room fades to black.

I hear my name being called and murmuring around me. Where am I? I blink my eyes open. Mr Bell is there, then another familiar face, Cooper, is leaning over me, frowning.

"Heidi... Heidi." He says in the gentlest voice I've ever heard. I hear someone say, "She's coming around."

Oh god, I didn't. Did I faint? My stomach churns as I try to sit. Please don't let me be sick.

Mr Bell supports me as I sit up, slowly dying inside, I want to be anywhere but here. We don't have earthquakes in England, but if we did, just a little one, that would be okay.

"I'm okay." My voice cracks and someone hands me a glass of water. I take a sip and eye Cooper over the glass.

He turns to the teacher. "Shall I take her to the nurse?"

Mr Bell does not know what to do.

Oh no. I shake my head. "It's fine, I'll be fine in a minute. It's happened before." Feeling a little more normal, I go to stand.

Mr Bell assesses me before turning to Cooper. "Are you sure?"

He shrugs. "No problem." He turns to me, "Come on, can you get up?"

I stand but my legs are wobbly as we walk outside. His arm slides around my back to support me. Okay legs. Hold up, you can do this.

I take a deep breath and walk with him toward the nurse's office.

After a few steps, when I have my balance, I turn to him, "I'm fine now, thanks, I can make it to the nurse on my own."

"I'm taking you," he says firmly.

Okay, so I guess he's taking me. Rescuing me twice in a week is not good for my crush on him and most definitely bad for my mortification.

He waits outside while I get checked over by the nurse. She knows me because Mum and I have had meetings with her because of my panic attacks, but thankfully she doesn't make a big deal of that when she sees Cooper with me. It is the first time I've ever had to see her for fainting. It's happened a couple of times at home but never at school. The nurse confirms what I knew: I'm fine, my vitals are fine. I knew it was a lack of oxygen because of my panic attack. Bloody panic attacks, I hate them. When are they going to stop controlling my life? They are an entity of their own, controlling my body. When am I going to get control?

The nurse goes to the main office to call Mum. I have to go home because of the fainting, even though I'm fine. She leaves the door open as she leaves and I see Cooper leaning on the wall, ankles crossed, in his jeans and t-shirt, his bag by his feet. It's not fair that sixth formers get to wear their own clothes while we have to wear full uniform. He's unaware that I can see him standing there, scrolling through his phone. Something else unfair, that sixth formers can have their phones as long as they're not in a lesson. Immediate detention for us if we're caught doing that.

"You don't have to be here," I say.

He looks up and those brown eyes bore into mine. "The nurse knew you."

"Pardon?"

"The nurse, she recognised you - are you ill?" He sounds concerned, coming to the wrong conclusion.

I shake my head, "No, nothing like that, I'm fine."

"But she does know you?"

I nod, "Yeah."

"Well?"

"It's personal."

He shrugs as though he doesn't care, but his eyes say something else. "Fair enough." He goes back to his phone.

I have the urge to tell him, I'm not sure why. I don't like the way he's assessing me, as though I'm weird and he can't suss me out - would he see me any better when he finds out that my stupid anxiety is taking over my life?

Probably not, but at least it explains why I can't talk to him.

"Cooper?"

His eyes meet mine, but he doesn't speak, and I motion for him to come inside the nurse's office. He sits down and waits for me to speak.

I stare at my hands, my fingers tapping something out as usual. "I have panic attacks."

"What?"

"Panic attacks, a lot of them, it's a problem. You've probably noticed that, well, I'm a little shy."

He raises his eyebrows. "You weren't shy on Friday."

I gasp, "You can't count that. I can't believe you brought that up, it doesn't count as usual behaviour."

He shakes his head but has a hint of a smile on his face. "I'm sorry, that was out of order, you weren't yourself."

"No, I wasn't. I had anxiety that started at primary school, but it's gotten worse - the Doctor says as I get older, I'm putting more pressure on myself. I have techniques to keep the panic attack at bay but sometimes it takes hold of me, and today it took me by surprise."

"Because you saw me." Why won't he stop looking at me? Oh yeah, because we're having a conversation. Damn social convention.

I wince, "Yeah, sorry."

He tilts his head. "But why?"

"Does it matter?" I ask.

"Well, yeah, if it's something I can change to make you feel better, I will."

That is so nice of him. I need him to stop being nice. The more feelings I get for him, the more nervous I will get. I need to be honest. If I'm honest, maybe I can get a handle on it. I told him I liked him on Friday for god's sake, yeah, I was drunk but he'll know I wasn't making it up. *Just tell him, Heidi.*

"You make me nervous," I say to the floor.

"How? I've never done anything to you."

"You don't need to, it's me that's the problem, not you."

"I get you're shy, but with me, I think it's more than that."

I don't want to carry on with this conversation. I close my eyes. Lying is the only way to go here. "It's guys in general."

"But not my brother," he says, flatly.

"No, he's my friend, and Harper's boyfriend now. It's guys I don't know, one's I find intimidating."

"What do you find intimidating about me?"

I snort – not the sexiest sound in the world!

I answer. "How about everything?"

"I'm sorry I make you feel that way. I can be intense, but I don't want to make anyone feel a certain way because of things I do, or how I come across." He says softly.

"It's not your fault, I don't even know you. It's my stupid brain and how it works."

How weird that I'm telling him this when I usually can't talk to people about it, but it's all pouring out.

"Is that why you play? To help?"

I nod, "Yeah, it calms me."

He nods, "I get that, the drums do that for me."

"You're good, I've heard you."

"So are you."

We stare at each other. I actually hold his gaze for more than five seconds.

"I love Guns N' Roses," he says, smiling.

My cheeks redden. "Me, too."

Something passes between us that I don't understand, and the nurse walks back in the room. She stops in her tracks and eyes us, her head flitting between us both. I suppose it seems a little cosy in here.

He stands and shakes his head. "I need to get going, will you be okay?"

I nod and within seconds he's gone.

Whatever just happened between the two of us, it was important. He was understanding me... we were understanding each other.

Chapter Six

Cooper

I arrive at the assembly hall. Mr Bell asked whoever he could to help with this show and none of us could say no. Not that I mind, to be honest. If it's to do with music, I'm in. I live and breathe music, rhythm, and beats, so if helping here means more of that, I'll do it. Nothing to do with the fact that Heidi will be here. Nothing at all. Nope. Even though those honey eyes of hers hypnotise me. She is terrified of me, I remind myself. She fainted because she saw me. It can't get much worse than that, so not sure why she's on my mind so much.

I throw my bag on the floor as she walks in. Her guitar hangs from her shoulder on a strap as she scans the room. Her eyes land on mine. She gives me a small smile, and my pulse quickens. She is the sweetest thing. If I was a normal guy, like my brother, I might like her, maybe ask her out. But I'm not. The last thing I would ever want to do is be accountable to someone and have to consider their feelings. No thanks. I'm happy just to think about myself. No one else.

Someone so shy that she can't even be in the same room as me without fainting, well that would be an interesting relationship. I'll pass. Still, she is so pretty and nothing like the girls at this school, she's different and that is a big deal for me. The way girls feel they have to conform a certain way, dress, do their hair, their make up the same. Why can't they just be who they want to be? I don't get it. Harper is getting it, but it's taken a while for her to get there, but Heidi, she's naturally herself, I doubt she could be any other way. Individuality oozes out of her. The way she dresses and stands. It's ironic that she has no confidence because she is the one girl at this school that has the guts to be herself. And God, the way she can play – she is impressive. I am such a perfectionist, but listening to her play, she sounded note perfect.

Sometimes I wish I was more like my brother, normal. But I have to deal with the cards life dealt me. Normal I'm not.

She walks over to me, without meeting my gaze, of course.

"Hey. Thanks for taking care of me last Wednesday." She has avoided me since, after telling me about herself. It took guts to tell me, and I respect that.

I shrug. "It's fine, no problem. How are you?"

"I'm okay. So, Mr Bell said he wants us to work together."

"Did he?" This is the first I've heard of it. Unless... she can't be. "Wait, you're not the song writer, are you?"

She folds her arms as if protecting herself. "Maybe?"

"Bell said he wanted me to work with someone, but he didn't say who."

She nods and winces, "Yeah, it shocked me when I found out it was you. The universe keeps throwing us together these last couple of weeks."

"It seems that way. You write?"

She nods, "I do."

"Music or words?"

"Both."

"A girl full of hidden talents, aren't you?"

She blushes and glances at me. There's that bolt of lightning again, shooting through me. My head may say walk away when it comes to Heidi, but the rest of me screams yes.

"What about you? Music or words?" she asks.

I smirk, "I do both too. Guess we best get started, huh?"

Only forty-five minutes later and we've put together a decent base for a song already. She's a natural with the melody and I'm sure I impressed her with the words I came up with. Even I'm surprised by how easily it came together. I haven't enjoyed myself so much in ages.

But the part I'm most happy about? She started to relax in my company, something she didn't even realise she was doing - it's the music; I understand because I'm the same, as soon as I'm doing anything musical, I relax. It's the only time I'm at ease. She even laughed a couple of times. Not so much with the looking me in the eye, but we were studying the notebook. Baby steps. We created a decent melody, but we need to perfect the words. It needs work, we've only just started, but at least we've got something to work with.

Mr Bell shouts, "We need to pack up. Great start today, guys, we will put on quite a show. I'm excited."

I watch Heidi as she puts her things in her bag. She would love The Hideaway. Could I do it? Invite her into my space? My space where I get to be me? But it's all about the music with her and she's not gonna go around telling everyone.

I clear my throat. "Heidi, can I ask you something?"

"About the song?"

"Kind of. There's this place that I go." I glance around to check no one is listening, as though it's something illegal.

She stops what she's doing. I have to laugh. "It's nothing to worry about. I was thinking, we could use some practice together and I'm part of this group, a meetup place, for kids around our age who're mostly into music. You'd be so good at teaching the younger ones to play

- hell, even some of the older ones. There's a stage and instruments set up so that we can practise. We're forming a band..."

She shakes her head. "Oh no, sorry, no I can't do that."

"It's okay, I get that's not your thing, but it's somewhere we can go to work on this song. I'm a perfectionist and need it to be right, it would be good if we could spend extra time on it together. It's a cool place, you'd like it."

She nods and bites her lip but that makes my eyes go to her mouth, "I guess."

"Do you want to come one night? With me?"

She shakes her head. "Dad would never let me."

I frown. "Why not?"

"Well, because of the party. He's been told what happened, but he has it in his head that we're covering for you. I mean, why would we even do that if you were the one to get me drunk? It doesn't make any sense, but he won't listen. I'm sorry he's so stubborn. He said I'm to have nothing to do with you. I had to plead with him not to mention your name at school, the only reason he didn't is because my mum was on my side too."

Is she serious? "Wait, you're telling me that because I helped you that night, when there was no one else, that now you're not even allowed to talk to me?"

"I'm sorry. It's ridiculous. He gets like this; he gets something in his head and no one can change it."

"This is a load of crap. What was I supposed to do, leave you there?" I'm beginning to hate her dad.

Her eyes widen, "God no, I'm so grateful that you came for me, that you took care of me. You carried me inside, which I am mortified about, by the way. You could have told Harper no, but you didn't, you took care of me."

"Yeah, seems like it wasn't worth the effort." As soon as those words leave my mouth, I feel terrible, that was out of order.

She bites her lip, tears welling in her eyes, "I'm sorry you regret it."

What an arse I am. "That was a dick thing to say. I didn't mean it, sorry."

"I don't blame you. I'm not worth the effort." Her voice breaks.

"Don't twist my words, Heidi, that's not what I meant, and you know it."

She shakes her head, "Sorry, Mum is working on him. It doesn't matter how tiny she is, she always gets her way. She will convince him he's wrong. There's no proof, so he has to take our word for it. Don't tell anyone that he's being like this - it's so embarrassing."

I get an idea. "What if we found out who did it? Have you got anywhere with that?"

She shakes her head. "No, the police don't have any evidence so it's just something I have to forget."

"Has any guy asked you out and you said no, or anything like that?"

She laughs. "Nooooo," she trails off, "Well, one did, but he wouldn't do anything like that."

"Was he at the party?"

She bites her lip, "I'm not sure."

"Maybe worth finding out?" If we can find out who did it, it would put her mind at ease and get her dad off my case.

She shakes her head, "No, I'm sure it was just something someone did to have a laugh at my expense."

I shrug, "Maybe, but I would be on my guard if I was you."

Her eyes flash with fear. "Yeah, I'm never anything else, thanks."

"So, we can't ever work on this out of school?"

She bites her lip, "Unless... unless I don't tell him I'm meeting you."

I shake my head, "No, don't do that, it would cause trouble."

She sighs, "I'll talk to Mum, see if she can talk some sense into him. Where is this place?"

"It's called The Hangout on Denman Street. Have you heard of it?"

She shakes her head.

"Not many have, but that's why I like it. It's not busy, only unsociable types like me hang there."

She tilts her head to one side in such a cute way.

Wait, stop thinking she's cute!

"How did you hear about it?" she asks.

"I had an instructor to help me with the drums and he knew of this place, he hangs out there sometimes."

She nods and gives me a smile. "You love playing, don't you?"

"I love anything musical. Nice to shut yourself away sometimes, right?"

She stares at me for a moment before she says, "Right."

We head out of the hall together and go our separate ways. I knew I'd miss the bus tonight, so I brought my car. "Do you want a lift home?"

She shakes her head, "I'd better not."

"Honestly? It's safer to walk home on your own than get in a car with me?"

"Depends, are you asking me or my dad?" She smirks.

"You."

"Can you drop me off on the corner of my street?"

I sigh, "Sure. Come on."

I can't deny that I want to spend more time with her. She's like the female version of me, which sounds weird, but when you meet someone on your wavelength you're bound to be drawn to that person. That's all it is. I'd love to introduce her to the guys at The Hideaway. Going there has helped me so much. It's obvious she needs something to escape. I'll have to introduce her to it without me being there. She wouldn't be interested in joining our band. Not that it's much of a band without a singer.

If only she could sing...

Chapter Seven

Heidi

As I walk up my path, my phone beeps with a text:

Sara: You better spill right now girl, I saw you!

Oh god, did she see me getting out of Cooper's car? So much for keeping out of sight.

Me: What are you talking about?

Sara: You better get here right now.

Me: I haven't had dinner yet. Come over later?

Sara: Oh, I will. Be there in an hour.

She is going to be disappointed when she arrives that it was all very innocent. I can't help feeling a flutter of excitement that I had a ride home in Cooper's car. Chatting to him, watching him drive...I had to force myself to face forward and not watch him.

I step inside and shout, "Mum!"

"In here." It's Dad's voice.

I walk into the living room, they're both sitting on the couch. Dad is on his laptop and mum is watching her tablet, wearing headphones.

She takes them off when she sees me. Dad asks, "How was school?"

"It was good, Mr Bell asked me to be part of a music production."

Mum raises her eyebrows. "Singing or guitar?"

"Oh my god, Mum, neither! Like I could ever... I'm helping write the songs and helping backstage, Mr Bell knows better than to ask me to perform."

She chuckles, "I guess so. How's the anxiety been today?"

"Great, actually! I enjoyed writing this song and yeah, been good all day."

Dad sighs, "All in your head anyway, love. You might hate me for saying it, but you're the one that's got to beat it, no point in all this fuss."

I roll my eyes. He has no idea.

Mum narrows her eyes at him, "Francis, stop it! How many times do I have to tell you? Don't talk about something you know nothing about. If she had the flu, would you tell her to get over it because it's in her head? No, you wouldn't. It's an illness, how many times do I have to tell you? And if you'd watch the videos and read the articles that the therapist gave us, you'd understand."

"Here we go again," Dad sighs. I love him, I do, but he can't get his head around this and if I'm honest, it hurts.

He is basically saying that I'm being dramatic. The guy that raised me has that opinion of me, what will everyone else's opinion be?

I walk out, saying, "I'm taking a shower and getting changed before dinner."

My phone goes again with a text:

Harper: Why is Cooper asking for your number?

My stomach lurches. Oh my god. He wants my phone number? The guy who I've crushed on for years is asking for my phone number. I feel sick, but excited sick.

Me: We're working on a song together for a music show, that's all. You can give it to him.

Harper: Oh boring, thought it was something juicy.

Me: Sorry to disappoint.

I wish it was something juicy! Jumping in the shower, he's all I think about. Cooper is going to text me. This Hideaway place sounds perfect, a place where I can enjoy music - my own kind of therapy. It would be nerve-wracking at first, meeting new people, but it would be good for me. And Cooper would be there. Gorgeous, sexy, hot Cooper.

I'd have to get around my dad first. I wonder if I speak to Mum, if she would cover for me?

Or...

I could do something I've never done before... keep something from them. I'm a terrible daughter for even thinking it, but if Dad wasn't being so unreasonable, I wouldn't need to lie. Telling Mum isn't an option either, she will tell Dad.

While washing my hair, I decide that if he texts me, I'm gonna tell him I spoke to Mum and she said I could go. Cooper was innocent and Dad is being unreasonable, and Cooper would make sure I get home safe. The thought of meeting with him out of school, in my own clothes, gives me butterflies. What could I wear? Who am I kidding, I only own three outfits, different combinations of skinny jeans and fitted t-shirts. I could tell Mum I'm going to Harper's as long as I don't get too dressed up, so her suspicions aren't raised. And she lives next door to Cooper so if Dad picks me up, I'd make sure I was back by then.

Guilt washes over me. I shouldn't be doing this. But I want to see Cooper out of school and want to be with people who understand me. That's not unreasonable, surely?

My phone is ringing as I get out of the shower. It's him! I run to answer it, then let out a sigh. It's only Harper. We chat about Cooper wanting my number and other stuff and I try to get rid of the disappointment that it isn't him.

Checking my phone a thousand times doesn't help, I still don't hear from him. Sara comes over so I tell her what she's missed. I tell her about The Hideaway, and she says I should go. Guess it's up to me to wrestle with the guilt. Even though, I've already decided I'm going to do it. I'll talk to Mum in the meantime and try to convince her to agree to it, even though I'm already going.

I'll tell him at school tomorrow, excited now that I've made the decision to go.

I'm falling asleep when my phone beeps with another text. Aren't I popular tonight? I check the time, it's 10.30.

Unknown number: Hey, it's Cooper, I hope it's okay to text you. I asked Harper for your number.

Me: Hey Cooper, yeah, it's fine, she told me she gave it to you.

Cooper: Now that we have each other's number, if either of us gets an idea for the song we can message.

My heart sinks that he's being purely business, but hey, at least I'll have his number in my phone.

Me: Yeah, that's a good idea. I had fun today.

Cooper: Me too.

Me:I'd like to come to that place if the offer's still open?

Cooper: Great! Did you talk to your parents?

Oh god, what should I say? Should I lie to him? It's only a white lie. He'd never agree to it if he thought I was going behind my parents' back. I type before I change my mind.

Me: Yeah, Mum agreed to it.

I cringe as I hit send. I hate lying, but I'm desperate to go. This is my dad's fault.

Cooper: That's brilliant, still need to win your dad over but great that you've got your mum on your side. Do you want to go tomorrow?

Oh my god. Tomorrow? I thought I'd have time to build up to it, talk myself into it. Should I say no?

I must take too long because he messages again;

Cooper; Have you fallen asleep?

Come on, Heidi, you have to go.

Me; No, I'm still here, tomorrow is good. What time?

Cooper; I'll pick you up at six, we can stay for a couple of hours, is that okay? I can bring you home.

Hmmm, Mum and Dad will see him picking me up and dropping me off. What should I do? Okay, gonna need to confide in Harper because I'll need her for this.

Me; It's okay, am going to Harper's after school, so can we go from there?

Cooper; Perfect.

I'm sure Harper will be fine with it, as long as she doesn't have plans... How will I get back home? I know! There's a shop on the corner of my street, I can tell him I need to buy something and to drop me off there. God, this lying thing is already exhausting, and I've not even done anything yet. Dad might drop me off as long as I don't mention Cooper goes. I'll cross that bridge when I come to it - I may not even like the place.

Me; Thanks for inviting me, it sounds great.

Cooper; You will like it, it could help you.

I frown and message back.

Me; Help me with what?

Does he think I'm a terrible guitar player? He said he thought I was good. I *know* I'm good.

Cooper; Well, you're shy right?

I swallow and reply.

Me Yeah, I guess. But I can't go on forever like this, can I?

Cooper; You just need to realise that who you are is absolutely fine.

It's as though someone has wrapped me in a warm blanket, a warm blanket of Cooper's words.

Me; Easier said than done but thank you for saying that.

Cooper; Thank you for telling the truth?

He is so sweet. Who'd have thought Cooper could be sweet? Although I'm not sure he's trying to be. I think he genuinely is telling the truth how he sees it.

Me; Yeah. Good night.

Cooper; Night, Heidi.

No kisses, but hey, I can't expect a miracle. Here's hoping for a smiley face next time.

I lay my head on my pillow with thoughts of what it must be like to watch Cooper playing the drums, what a sight that would be. What will tomorrow night bring?

I fall asleep, proud of myself that I'm pushing myself out of my comfort zone - let's hope I don't completely make a fool of myself so that he wishes he'd never invited me.

Chapter Eight

Heidi

I spot Cooper from the other side of the yard, making his way towards me in that cool way of his. Walking as though he has all the time in the world and doesn't care about anything. I could watch him do that all day long. It's like reading a good book - you never want it to end. He's wearing dark jeans and a hoody with a leather jacket over the top. He has his hair closely cropped, and it suits him and his no-nonsense personality. Those brown eyes fix on me, making my belly tie in knots. He is so handsome.

Harper and I are sitting eating lunch. She leans in. "Cooper is coming over. I'm certainly seeing a lot more of him lately."

I mock scowl at her and look Cooper's way, smiling.

He reaches us and throws his sandwich on the bench, sitting himself opposite us.

Harper speaks, "Cooper, to what do I owe this honour?"

Oh god, I haven't told her about tonight yet, she's gonna make a big deal of it. What if he mentions it? Crap!

He glances at her and rolls his eyes. "You don't have the honour. I'm here to speak to Heidi."

She nods, "Thought so. You see your brother on your travels?"

He rolls his eyes, "Yeah, don't worry he will be here soon, can't you live without him for more than five minutes?"

"Shut up, we're in love," Harper snaps.

He shakes his head as though disgusted. "Yeah, you live at our house these days."

"Aw, you jealous cos I'm stealing your brother's attention?" She smiles at him sickly sweet.

He snorts, "Harper, you have always stolen my brother's attention. It's not as though we're inseparable, is it?"

"Whatever, anyway, what do you want my Heidi for?"

"To talk about tonight."

Harper's eyeing me, "What's happening tonight?"

Like a deer caught in headlights, I freeze. What do I do now?

I open my mouth to answer when Edward and Liam appear. They're engrossed in conversation, probably about basketball, they both play on the school team.

They reach us and say 'hi'. Edward goes straight to Harper and sits on the edge of the bench, sliding his arm around her shoulders and kissing her on the lips. They are so cute together and it's like they've been seeing each other for years. That's what happens when best friends fall in love, they're comfortable with each other. What would it be like to be so comfortable with a guy that you can be completely yourself? I'm so happy for her that she has that.

Ed looks at Cooper. "What are you doing here?"

Cooper sighs and runs his hands over his head. He glances my way.

I speak. "He wanted to talk to me about something we're doing together for the show."

Check me out, being brave enough to talk in a group of boys.

Ed nods but looks at Cooper for longer than he needs to and raises his eyebrows, but Cooper doesn't acknowledge him. He asks me, "Still on for tonight?"

I nod and concentrate a little too intently on unwrapping my sandwich. "Yeah, of course."

He smirks and gets on with eating his sandwich. Why can't I be normal around him? I hate myself sometimes. How am I supposed to eat in front of him? I'm gonna choke!

I take small nibbles and try to seem comfortable, but I'm hyper-aware that he's sitting opposite me. Why does he look so good chewing when I'm imitating a hamster trying to get through a lettuce?

Thank God Harper didn't have plans and she was fine with me coming to hers. Crisis averted. She understands my dilemma but thinks I should tell my mum.

I'll think about it, but not tonight - tonight there are other important things to think about. My outfit. I wear my light blue ripped skinny jeans and a *Guns'N'Roses* t-shirt with my Doc Martens. It's my favourite pair of jeans that show off what little curves I have the best. My figure is okay, I have boobs and a waist, and I'm at peace with what I've got. I leave my freshly washed hair wavy and wear my signature glasses, because without them I can't see a thing. I put blusher and lip gloss on but leave it at that, I don't want Mum or Dad to notice and ask questions.

Harper waits with me in her living room, sitting on the edge of her couch, assessing me. "Heidi, I know what you're like, you're all worked up, you need to relax."

I arrived at hers around half an hour ago and have been on pins. She is right, I feel like a stick of dynamite and the wick is right at the end.

"Oh yeah, can you tell me how?" I check my phone for the hundredth time, waiting for 6 o'clock.

"Let's talk about something else," Harper suggests.

"Something other than going to a place where I don't know anyone, with a boy that intimidates me, that is gorgeous? And something other than me trying to do things I've never done before?"

She sighs, "Yeah, anything but those topics."

"What will he do? Will he text me to go outside?" I ask.

"Cooper will do anything to avoid conversations in person, so yeah, you'll get a text."

Before I can answer, there's a knock at the front door. Harper opens it, "Hey, gorgeous." Ed says as he barges in the room. He turns to me. "Cooper is getting in his car, he says to tell you to go and get in."

Such a gentleman - not - but I guess this isn't a date. At all.

"See you guys later." The night air is cool as I make my way outside, giving me goosebumps. At least I think it's that and not the thought of being next to Cooper on our drive.

He's sitting in his car, the engine running. While smoothing down my top, I try to magic up something witty to say.

"You ready for this?" he asks as I climb into the passenger seat.

"Not at all, but no pain no gain, right?"

He concentrates on the road while he talks, "Why pain? It will not be painful, I promise, once you've been there five minutes you will relax - you'll be surrounded by like-minded people."

"Let's hope my anxiety doesn't take over."

He glances at me, "Are you going to faint again?"

I laugh, nervously, "No, not yet." Funnily enough, I feel fine. I'm nervous, my stomach is in knots, but I haven't got the tightness in my chest that I normally do.

"You'll be fine."

Why, I don't know, but Cooper's presence relaxes me. Maybe it's because he's so laid back.

The huge hall we walk into is nothing like I imagined. It's more like a nightclub than a hall, with its dim lighting and plush couches around the edges. There are spotlights towards one end and instruments set up. An older guy sits at a desk in the corner, working on a laptop. A group of three girls sit at a table and when we walk in, they halt their conversation. There are vending machines of different varieties and a kitchen behind them.

One girl breaks off from the three and walks toward us.

I take a deep breath. Come on, Heidi, you can do this. Don't be a weirdo.

The girl smiles at me, she has long brown hair in two plaits. She is a petite little thing. "Hey, Cooper, who's this?"

"Hey, Jen, this is Heidi, I told her about this place - she's into music, so she wanted to see what we're about," Cooper answers.

"Aw cool, nice to meet you Heidi, any friend of Cooper's is a friend of ours. Come in, make yourself at home."

I smile at her and relax my shoulders. This isn't so bad. "Thanks, nice to meet you too and I'll try, I'm a little nervous around new people." It's best to be honest; if I'm not, my shyness can be interpreted as being a bitch. It's happened before, so best to explain early.

Jen laughs, "Oh you'll be right at home here, we're all a little socially awkward. You'll see, it'll soon become your favourite place."

I'm not sure, but even though I don't know Cooper that well, I feel as though he gets me. If Cooper likes these people, maybe they will get me too. Could Cooper be socially awkward too, like me, and it comes across as arrogance? I look over at him, suddenly seeing him in a different light.

Cooper raises his eyebrows at me. "Come on, I'll introduce you to the boss."

Then he does something that makes my heart stop. He grabs my hand to guide me with him. His hand wraps around mine. His skin touches my skin. And boy does my skin know it. It feels like I've been electrocuted and wrapped in a warm fluffy blanket at the same time. I want to freeze time. How my feet work I do not know, but they do. They follow him of their own accord separate from my brain.

"Derek, this is Heidi, she plays - and I mean *plays* - electric guitar."

Derek looks to be in his late forties. He has glasses which he fiddles with as he speaks.

"Nice to meet you, Heidi - always great to see fresh faces. Can you fill in your details?" He grabs an iPad, pressing a few buttons before handing it to me. "There you go, for health and safety blah blah, the boring stuff."

"Okay, no problem. Is there a fee for coming here?"

He waves his hand. "No fee, I get a government grant that covers the bills, you just need money for a drink or snack if you want one."

I nod, "That's brilliant. Thank you so much. This place is great."

He smiles at me and eyes Cooper, "So, how do you two know each other?"

"We're in a music show at school together. I've heard her play, Derek, you won't believe it. She's shy though, but she's working on it, right, Heidi?"

I smile at him and nod. Who knew he could be this sweet?

Derek nods and smiles, "That's brilliant. Maybe the singer for your band?"

He chuckles, "No, she doesn't sing." He turns to me. "Do you?"

I shake my head but keep quiet. I *do* sing, I can sing fine, but not in front of people. No way I'm admitting that.

Another lie, Heidi, you're getting to be quite the professional.

Derek carries on, "Maybe you can give a couple of lessons once you've settled in? No performing, but tutoring, maybe? Anything that these guys can do to give them a skill would be good and, come on, electric guitar is *the* coolest instrument."

"Hey, drums win that one!" Cooper says.

Derek shakes his head and looks to me. "He has no idea."

I wonder what that means; does he play?

"I'd be happy to tutor." I'm pleased that I can help a guy who will do this for kids.

Cooper's eyes are shining. He rarely seems relaxed, but he's relaxed and at home right here. "Do you want a drink?"

I nod, my mouth dry with nerves. "Sure." I follow him to the vending machine, and we walk over to the stage.

He points to the drums. "We set my kit up there. Mum bought it and donated it. They didn't want to hear me playing at home. Mum says two teenage boys are loud enough without putting drums into the mix."

"That's so good of them. They're supportive, huh?"

Something flashes across his face that I can't fathom, did I hit on a touchy subject? "Yeah, kind of, as long as it's just for fun. What about yours?"

As long as it's just for fun. Hmmm, may be a conversation there.

I sidestep that for now—I need to know him better before I delve into that. "Yeah, mine are supportive, surprisingly, they let me take lessons at home, and they bought me my last guitar for Christmas."

"Why 'surprisingly'?"

I shrug. "They can be intense, but they let me have this one."

"That's cool." He points to a guitar case in the corner. "Feel like playing?"

My eyes widen. Will anyone be watching us? There are still the three girls at the table and the guy in the corner. I'm not sure I can.

He shakes his head, "Sorry, I shouldn't have asked, it's fine. Let's go sit over there and work on our song."

Something bubbles inside me. He's writing me off, expecting that I can't do it.

There are four strangers here. I should do it... he has presumed that I can't, time to prove him, and myself, wrong...

Come on, Heidi, you want to be a rock chick, time to start.

"Why not? Let's give it a go."

He raises his eyebrows. "Really? You don't have to."

I shrug as if it's no big deal when inside I'm screaming 'Nooooo!', "Yeah, why not? It's not like there's a room full of people, right? These guys don't know me, and you've already heard me play."

His eyes light up. "Well yeah, if you're sure. Let's do one track together, see how you feel, no pressure, okay? What do you know?"

No pressure, yeah right. I tilt my head to one side, trying to think of a song that I know inside out, "Well, what do *you* know?"

"Everything." His eyes are twinkling; he's having fun. I like this playful side of him.

I tap my hands on my lips. Hmmm, what to play? Is it wrong that I really want to impress him? "Yeah, course you do. What about Nirvana?"

He raises his eyebrows, "*Smells Like Teen Spirit?*"

"Any."

He shakes his head. "You never fail to surprise me."

I blush, liking that I've impressed him. "Come on then, let's have a go."

We walk to the side steps and climb up onto the stage. I search for the darkest corner that my guitar cord will allow. I can do this. This is where I have to force past the nausea.

He points to the amp. "The amp will be plugged in."

"Whose guitar is this? Should I be using it?" I'm protective over my guitar, so I imagine whoever owns this is the same. I don't want to upset someone.

He shouts to Derek, "Derek, can Heidi use your guitar?"

He is on his phone but gives the thumbs up.

"It's Derek's?" He keeps getting cooler and cooler.

He nods, "Yeah and I'm guessing it'll be tuned to perfection."

I open the case and catch my breath. Wow, this is quite the guitar. It's worth a fortune. I look at Derek who is watching me, smiling. He can read my mind.

My full attention goes back to the guitar and I stroke it gently, it's stunning. I pick it up and slide the strap over my shoulder sinking into the sensation of holding it. The model I own is decent, but this is something else.

Something that is way too expensive for me to be playing. Cooper's eyes are on me as I walk over to him. I try not to notice how hot he looks sitting at his drum kit but fail. He's hot anyway, but sitting at a drum kit with drumsticks in his hands? Wow.

I lean into him, "This guitar will have cost a fortune. I'm scared to even touch it."

He grins, "Derek is a millionaire, he's loaded. He bought this place outright because he didn't have anywhere to go when he was growing up around here. So yeah, he's rich, and he plays, so no way he'd get an average model."

"How is he so sure everyone will treat it well?"

He shrugs, "He trusts people, and they give him their respect. Everyone who comes here thinks highly of him. He's cool."

I decide I love Derek. How cool of him to set this up and give his time to come here.

I plug in my guitar and switch on the amp. Even the buzz of the amp calms me. I check the room - no one is watching. I strum the strings and calmness and belonging washes over me. The. Best. Feeling. Ever.

Cooper is watching me and smiling. He raises his eyebrows as if to say 'ready?'.

I nod, "You counting down?"

"Sure... three, two, one." And the beat of his drums starts. I come in with my notes and we play. What a feeling. We sound amazing together. I know this song like the back of my hand. Most of the songs I've learned, I know by heart because I've practised each one of them over and over again. Plus, I seem to have a photographic memory, but only with music. Once I've played something a couple of times, I remember it.

We play as though we've practised together for years. He is amazing, so talented and like me, he comes alive when he plays. At the end of the track, the girls on the table start clapping and Derek whoops. The embarrassment sets in but I'm on a high. It's the best buzz in the world. The first time I've played in front of people, and they liked it! Hooray! And I did it with Cooper. Hot, sweet, sexy Cooper. We have just bonded over something that so many people won't ever get. But he does. He gets it. He gets me.

I turn to Cooper, flushed. "That was... that was fab!"

He nods grinning widely, a sheen of sweat on his forehead, "Another one?"

I glance at the girls and back to him, "I'm not sure... they listened." I whisper.

He throws his head back and laughs and what a sight to behold. "You played the guitar like a pro and it's not a quiet amp. Of course they're gonna listen. But you were brilliant, and they liked it. Come on, why stop there... another one?"

I nod, reluctantly, "Fine, you pick."

He glances away and then back at me with a wicked grin. God, I love him like this. "Know any U2?"

I roll my eyes, playfully, "Would I even be a guitar player if I didn't?"

He chuckles. "Still haven't found?"

I nod. "One of my favourites."

We hold each other's eyes for longer than needed as something passes between us, I break off and take my position, ready to play. And play we do.

All too soon it's time to go home. I get what he means about this place. It homey, I've found somewhere I belong and can't wait to come back. Why didn't I find this place sooner? We played four songs together and then thought we'd better give the other guys in the room a break - we were being loud - so we worked on the words of our song. This part was harder for me than the melody. I loved spending time with him, just chatting, he did his best to put me at ease and when we had a break, he bought me a diet Pepsi from the vending machine. Is it wrong that I want to keep the empty bottle and use it as an ornament for my room? Then, every time I see it, I'll remember this incredible night. He will never realise what he has done for me, bringing me here.

We grab our coats and he leans into me, "I need the loo, be back in a minute."

I nod and go by the door to wait. Jen comes over, "Hey, did you have fun?"

I smile, "Oh yeah, I've loved it, this place is amazing."

She nods, "It is. Don't tell me how, but it's like misfits make their way here and are at home."

My eyes widen, "That's what it feels like to me. I struggle, well, to talk to people." Why am I telling this to someone I just met?

She nods, "I get it, honestly, but you can relax here."

I smile at her. The other two girls have their attention on the men's room, waiting for Cooper to come out. She follows my gaze. "Yeah, some of the girls have a crush on Cooper. Tall brooding drum player? It's every girl's dream come true in this place."

I chuckle, "Yeah, I bet. What about you? Are you immune to his charms?"

She nods, "Yeah, I like my guys to be fun-loving, laugh a lot. One thing you never see Cooper doing is laughing... although I caught him laughing a few times tonight with you - the first time I've ever seen that. You two make a cute couple and you play together like you were made to."

Heat floods my body at the thought that everyone here presumes we're a couple. "Oh, we're not like that. We're friends, and he's helping me with my music."

"Girl, you don't need any help."

And again, I blush. Seriously... what's with the blushing?

"Thanks, but it's when I'm not behind a guitar that's the problem. I struggle talking to people."

She nods, "Now that I *do* see, but you get past that, overcome whatever is holding you back, and you could rock the world."

"Thank you, I'm working on it."

"Working on what?" Cooper arrives behind me.

Jen answers, "Working on stopping you from having a big head."

He rolls his eyes and turns to me. "Ready to go?"

Once we're on the road, I turn to him. "Thank you for taking me there. I had the best night I've ever had. I actually played in front of people - I mean, only five people, but this is huge for me. I didn't panic, in fact, I loved it. Once we'd played our first track, I swear I could have gone on forever." I'm babbling, I still haven't come down from my high.

He keeps his eyes on the road, but I see him smile. "You're welcome, you're an amazing player - you're talented."

I snort, "Yeah, but I need to get over the crippling stage fright."

"It's only the build-up. You need to work on that, because as soon as you start playing, you forget your nerves. It's mesmerising to watch. You're lost in the music."

"I am, but you're the same when you play. It's so great when you find something you love doing isn't it?"

"The best," he says quietly. Hmm, what's that about?

I stick to my plan and ask him to drop me off at the corner shop. He wants to wait until I've bought what I needed, but I convince him not to, on a promise that I'll text him when I get home. I hate lying to him and my parents, but after the night I've had, it's one hundred per cent worth it. As long as I don't get caught, who am I hurting?

I text him as soon as I get in my bedroom.

Me; Home safe. Thanks again, Cooper. With a big smiley face.

It's ten minutes before I get one back,

Cooper; You're welcome, I enjoyed spending time with you tonight.

I do a little dance around my bedroom when I read that.

Me; Good, cos I'll be coming to the hideaway again and again and again - you will regret showing me that place.

Cooper; I doubt it. Want to meet at lunch to work on the song?

Me; Sure.

Cooper; Okay, meet you at the usual bench, we'll eat with the gang and then go to music.

Me; Sounds good. Night Cooper.

Cooper; Sweet dreams.

Oh god, did he tell me to have sweet dreams? I didn't think I could fall for him any harder. This crush I've had on him since year nine has been getting worse and worse, but this past week? The way he's been with me, I can't get him out of my head. He's my every thought and he just told me to have sweet dreams.

Crushes are something else: we don't know the person, so we imagine them to be a certain way in our head. But since getting to know Cooper and finding out who he really is, my crush has been crushed, and a whole new infatuation has grown.

Mum walks into my bedroom seconds afterwards, making me feel, and look, really guilty. "Hey honey, did you have a good time tonight at Harper's?"

It is killing me that I can't tell her what I did. That I actually played in front of people. This monumental thing that happened to me and I have to keep it to myself. I need to tell her, but not tonight. I need tonight for just me.

"Yeah, it was good, Mum."

"How's your anxiety been today?"

"It's been good, no problems." Never thought I'd say that after I'd been on a stage.

"That's good, therapy tomorrow after school."

I nod, "Yeah, I think she'll be pleased."

She sighs. "I'm sorry that your dad finds it hard to understand."

"It's not your fault, Mum. It's not even his fault, he doesn't get it, doesn't understand how it feels. He has really upset me about Cooper. It's so embarrassing at school."

She frowns, "Are you sure it was innocent on his part?"

"Mum! Not you too?" I thought she would be on my side.

She shakes her head, "Well, you've never gotten in that state before, or even been in any kind of trouble before, and then this boy comes on the scene and you turn up drunk."

"I'm not going over this again. The reason he was on the scene is that he was *helping* me. Not trying to hurt me. I can't believe you think I'm lying."

She sighs, "I was a teenager once too."

"It hurts that you don't trust that I'm telling the truth. If my own parents don't believe me, what chance have I got?"

Guilt washes over me - I'm being a hypocrite. While I might be telling her the truth about this, I'm lying to her about where I've been tonight.

Her eyes widen, "I know you're telling the truth, but you don't have a clue what was happening, you were too out of it."

I flop back onto my bed, "I don't want to talk about this. Cooper is innocent and with the way you've both treated him, he may never help another girl again."

"I'm sorry. I can't help thinking the worst about a teenage boy."

"Yeah, I've noticed. Just try, Mum? Please?"

She nods and blows me a kiss, "I will. Night, sweetheart."

I try to breathe out my anger after she leaves. How can she judge someone so quickly? No way am I telling her now. I can't believe her. I shake my head to get Mum out of my head. Cooper. He's the subject of my thoughts right now.

I close my eyes and images of Cooper playing the drums, lost in the rhythm, send me to sleep and give me the sweetest dreams. Just like wished for me.

Chapter Nine

♥

I go downstairs, ashamed to admit that there's a spring in my step. It's her. I can't stop thinking about her. I need to stop...get her out of my head. But Jesus, the way she played. She is amazing. I challenge any guy to watch her play and not feel something.

Why does she think she's the opposite of amazing? She could be on a stage with Ariana Grande performing in front of millions and still not believe she's good enough. I can see it in her eyes. What has made her feel that way about herself? I hate it.

I'm going to change the opinion that she has of herself if it's the last thing I do. Confidence is the only thing that's standing in the way of her success, and she has zero. Well, she will be the most confident girl I've never met by the time I'm done with her. I'm not the only one that sees she's amazing. Her friends love her and her mum is so supportive of her anxiety issues.

Anxiety.

Having panic attacks is something I know absolutely nothing about. I need to find out all the facts so that I can get how her brain works. I know she panics, and her body takes over so she can't control it. But I need to find out what causes that. I can either Google the hell out of it or ask someone. I really don't want to ask Harper, although she is the obvious choice. She would get suspicious and wonder why I'm showing so much interest in her friend. She will hound me to tell her why I care, I know she will. That's not something I do, showing people I care, even to the ones closest to me it doesn't come naturally. Harper is my only option at this point though; I'm guessing she gets it. She and Sara are her closest friends. Could I trust Harper not to say anything to Heidi? She's like my little sister, so I'll just threaten to make her life a misery if she says anything. Although with how loved up she is with my brother, if I even look at her the wrong way these days, he scowls at me. I'm happy that they're happy, but this togetherness crap makes me want to throw up.

I walk into the kitchen. Speak of the devil. Harper's here with Ed, waiting for the crumpets to pop from the toaster, standing close together and whispering. Mum is around somewhere. Dad is at work already.

"It's way too early to watch you two be all cosy cosy." Even I recognise how grumpy I sound.

Harper turns around and smiles at me, her eyes shining. She is so happy. A different girl from a few months ago, one that pretended to be happy, but my annoying brother is a big part of that. He makes her happy.

She tilts her head at me and grins. "Aw, you jealous? Do you want to be cosy cosy with someone?"

"Get lost. Do me a crumpet."

I sit at the kitchen table and start scrolling through my phone.

"Hey, don't talk to her like that," Ed says.

"Ed, she's like my sister... it's allowed."

"Yeah, but she's also my girlfriend, so you have to respect her."

She gazes at him, her eyes wide, and places a hand on his chest to reach up and kiss him quickly. "My hero."

I roll my eyes. "Ed, don't you need to get dressed?"

"Don't you need to get a personality?" he shoots back.

I lean back in my chair and smirk, "Dude, I'm happy with mine the way it is."

The crumpets pop and they both set about buttering them - because, of course, it's a two-person job.

My phone pings. My heart jumps when I see her name.

Heidi; Morning. Are we meeting at dinner still? I still can't believe I played last night - I'm so proud of myself!

I've noticed she finds it easier to open up on texts, which I get - I guess it's easier for me to talk on text too. I smile - she's happy this morning, I have something to do with that, and I like that.

"Who is that?" Harper asks, her eyes laser-focused on me.

"No one, why?" I put my phone face down so she can't see the screen.

Her eyes narrow on me. "You're smiling...you *never* smile."

"Yeah, I do, but when you're around, there's nothing to smile about." I give her a false grin.

"Hey! Leave her alone, I won't tell you again. If you don't, I'll have a word with Mum and Dad about where you keep disappearing off to."

He wouldn't dare. "What are you talking about? They know where I go."

"Kind of, yeah, but you've not talked to them properly about it, have you?" He raises his eyebrows. He knows he's got me.

I can't believe he's bringing this up in front of Harper. And now.

"Leave it, Ed."

He shakes his head and we have a little staring contest. He breaks it when he says, "I'm gonna go get dressed, think you can manage to be nice to her?"

My mouth goes dry; this is my chance. "Of course. Come here, little sis, sit with me." I pat the chair next to me and she walks over with her plate and sits, eyeing me warily.

Once he's left the room she turns to me, "Why do you wind him up like that? You're only mean to me in front of him to push his buttons. You're always nice to me when it's just us."

I shrug, "I can't help it, I find it funny."

She sighs, "So, who were you really texting?"

I study her. "How much can I trust you?"

"Ooh, this sounds good." She wriggles in her chair.

"I mean it. I want to talk to you about something, but only if I'm sure you won't repeat it."

She shakes her head. "If it's important and you ask me not to, I promise I won't say anything."

"You may want to, but you would screw things up for me if you did."

She places her hand on mine, "Hey, I won't. I promise you can talk to me, for what good I'll be. What's up?"

"It was Heidi texting me."

"I knew it!" she grins, slapping the table.

I shake my head, "Not like that. I mean, possibly like that. Maybe. How well do you know her?"

She frowns, "What do you mean?"

How do I put this? "Like...her issues."

"Her anxiety," she mumbles.

"Yeah, how bad is it?"

She winces, "It can be pretty bad. I feel for her, she tries to fight it so much but sometimes it takes control of her. I've seen it happen a lot. I wish I could help her. But she has lots of techniques and stuff and she still sees a therapist. She seems to be doing great at the moment."

A therapist. Wow, serious stuff. "I want to help her. Have you heard her play?"

"Yeah, she's ace, isn't she?" she pauses, "Wait. You've heard her play?"

I nod, "Yeah, last night, we played together."

Her eyes widen, "I never thought she'd agree to that."

"Why not?"

"She doesn't play in front of anyone ever - it's like her escape. Did she sing too?"

Wait...what? "She sings?"

She nods slowly, "Okay, so I guess she hasn't told you that part. Don't tell her I told you. She has the most amazing voice you've ever heard, sort of Amy Winehouse, Duffy kind of vibe. She's seriously good, but only me, her mum and Sara hear her mostly when she doesn't realise she's doing it. She's comfortable around us. I don't even think she's told Mr Bell."

"Why doesn't she realise how good she is?"

"She has anxiety, Cooper. It's an illness, you understand that, right?"

"Actually, no, that's why I wanted to talk to you. I want to help her. She's too good to keep it behind closed doors, and she can sing, too? She needs to be heard. But I don't know anything about mental health or panic attacks. Can you help me?"

She nods, "Sure, I'll email you some info. But it's not an easy cure where you can tell her she's brilliant and she's over it. You get that, right?"

I shake my head. "Of course, I get that." I kinda was hoping it would be that simple.

"Leave it to me." She sits back and watches me as though debating whether to say something.

"What?"

She winces, "There's something I want to tell you, but I really really can't, I'd be betraying her trust. So, I'll tell you this. Be careful with Heidi, she comes across as fragile but she's more fragile than you think. Be careful with her feelings."

My stomach lurches. "What do you mean by that?"

She shakes her head, "Let's say that she cares what your opinion is of her more than most."

What? Why?

I open my mouth to ask what she means, and she stands up, "Okay, said too much now. That's it."

Said too much? She hardly said anything!

She walks to the bottom of the stairs to shout to Edward to see if he's ready. I'm left feeling totally out of my depth. Should I get involved at all?

Chapter Ten

Heidi

I walk through the school gates happier to go to school than I have ever been in my life. I get to spend time with Cooper again today. We're even having lunch together. Some people could even call that a date! Not too many people, but still. He hasn't texted me back yet, but we made the arrangements last night anyway, he mustn't have seen his phone.

I've done my mindfulness app, and I'm all set for the day. It's my therapy session tonight, which is now once a month. She'll be happy with the progress I've made. I am. I'm proud of myself. I could conquer the world today.

I turn to Sara, "Today is going to be a great day."

She grins, "Yeah, I get it, you're happy that you are meeting with the hot sixth-former that you've liked in forever."

"What? No, I haven't." There's no way she could know I've been crushing on him, I never told anyone.

"You're seriously denying this to me? Your friend, who knows you inside out?" she rolls her eyes. "Even though you've never actually come out and said it, you've liked him for ages, ever since you found out he played the drums."

That makes me sound shallow! Plus, if I've been this transparent, does everyone know? "Yeah, I guess he really likes music."

"So, this makes him irresistible to you, does it?"

Is that wrong? Plus, that love of music comes wrapped in an extremely nice package.

"A little, yeah, if I'm honest. But he's interesting, he's not like the other boys."

"No, he always has a scowl on his face."

Yes, he does, his perfectly beautiful face. I smile to myself. That scowl has been dropping lately when he's with me.

I change the subject, even though I want to talk about him all day long. "I'm so excited for Alton towers on Friday, are you?"

Sara scrunches her face up. "Yeah, but I'm not sure I will go on all those huge vomit-inducing rides, but I will go for the little tea cup rides."

"I'm not a big fan of the hardcore stuff either, I will be right there on the tea cups with you. I can see the headlines now. Anxiety girl faints while upside down on the Thunderloop. Nah, I'll pass."

She rolls her eyes, linking me, "You are such a rock chick, will you teach me your cool ways when I'm older?"

I laugh, even I know I'm the opposite of a true rock chick.

I nudge her shoulder. "Shut up. Come on, let's go to registration."

I'm almost bouncing by lunchtime. I can't wait to see him, talk to him, stare at his lovely face. I make my way to our bench where we eat lunch. If one of our group gets there early enough, we save it. My luck is in; it's free and I'm the first one there, so I sit and open my packed lunch.

Rosie is the next to arrive. "Hey, Heidi, you good?" she smiles at me.

I nod, taking a bite, "Yeah, I'm trying to eat my lunch quick. Cooper is meeting me here to do some work for the music show."

I don't see Edward approaching behind me, but he hears what I say. "Oh, hasn't he texted you? He said he couldn't make it but that he'd text you."

My heart sinks right to the floor, dissolving into a pool of goo and slithering into the drain. Did he bail on me? I try to keep my voice normal and answer Edward. "Oh right, my phone isn't turned on. Why can he not make it?"

He shrugs, "Dunno, he said something came up. It's not a big deal, is it?"

I shake my head way too quickly, "No, not at all, it's no problem."

Edward gets distracted by the arrival of Harper. I study my sandwich. Did I do something bad last night? What happened? I thought he'd had fun, but maybe he was just being kind.

I can't help the crushing disappointment that floods through me. I sit quietly and nibble my food, wondering what the heck I did wrong.

I need to see if he sent me a text, but we're not allowed to turn our phones on, which he would have known, unless he texted me back this morning and thought I'd get it before I turned my phone off. I tell them I'm going to the toilet so I can check my phone. Was I being too full-on texting him this morning?

I get in a cubicle and turn on my phone, waiting for a message to come through. A few seconds later my phone vibrates. I read the message.

Cooper; Sorry something has come up. Will need to rearrange.

Doesn't matter how many times I read it; it comes across as abrupt. But that's the thing about messages, I guess we can interpret them any way you like, depending on your mood and the way your brain wants to. But in my current mood? There's only one way I'm gonna read it and that's badly. Very badly.

I take a deep breath and go back to find the gang. Harper sees me. "Where did you go? I thought you were meeting Coop?"

I shake my head, "Something came up, he had to cancel."

Something flashes in her eyes that I can't decipher.

"What?" I ask her.

She glances at Ed, but he is looking at her blankly, "No... nothing. I wonder what happened."

I shrug. "Dunno, no big deal, right?"

She nods her head slowly. "Sure."

Why is she being weird? I narrow my eyes at her, but she busies herself by talking to the others. I know her too well, she's hiding something. Has Cooper said something to her? Something I did wrong last night?

I can't cope with the knots in my stomach, I need find out. I stand, "Harper, can you come and help me with something for a second?"

She seems unsure but agrees and follows me to the other side of the yard, we stand next to the music building.

When we have our backs to the others, I turn and face her. "Okay, spill."

"What are you talking about?"

"Cooper has said something to you about me, hasn't he? Did I embarrass him last night?"

The familiar sensation of sickness builds in me as my heart rate picks up.

Oh god, what did I do?

"What? No, of course not." She won't look me in the eye.

"Please tell me, or I won't be able to face him ever again."

She sighs. I stand and watch her but remain silent. She'll crack.

"God, I'm so mad at Cooper for putting me in this position. Why did he have to cancel, anyway?" she mutters.

"That's what I'm asking you." I say slowly.

"He'll kill me if I say anything."

"I'll kill you if you don't." I cross my arms and glare at her.

"Okay, but he made me promise not to tell you. This morning he was asking me about you, he was asking about your anxiety."

I go cold all over, afraid where this is leading.

"What was he asking?"

"Things like, how can you think so little of yourself and what anxiety and panic attacks are because he doesn't understand them."

"So, you told him."

She nods, "Well, yeah, only what I know, not much, but he asked if I'd help him understand."

My stomach lurches. "So, he asked you about my panic attacks and why I'm a weirdo, then cancelled on me at lunch."

I'm fighting tears. I try to take a deep breath I don't want to get upset in front of Harper.

"No, I'm sure it's nothing to do with that. It's just a coincidence. See this is what you do, Heid, you automatically think the worst. You both had a great time last night and I'm pretty sure he likes you; he was asking me about you this morning, wanting to understand. He said he thinks you're awesome."

She bites her lip as though remembering something. "What?"

"Oh god, nothing, I may have accidentally mentioned that you can sing too. That has nothing to do with this, but seeing as I'm being honest, thought I'd better mention it so I don't get in trouble at a later date."

"Harper! No, why did you tell him?"

"He was saying how good you were, how you played with him, and I thought if you played in front of him you may have sung too."

I could actually kill this girl. I shake my head, "No way could I ever do that. Anyway, doesn't matter now. You told him about my problems, and he cancelled. You think I'm being negative? Well, let's see."

I walk away, needing five minutes on my own. I rush into the music block, somewhere I'm comfortable. I need to get my head sorted out. As I walk into the main music room, Cooper is there, staring at me.

I see that the window is open at the side of him. Well, this just went from bad to worse.

"You heard."

He nods. "So, trusting Harper is a big no."

I need to get out of here. I turn to go back the way I came.

"Heidi, wait!"

I shake my head and grab the handle to pull the door open, but as quick as a flash he's there behind me, keeping the door shut with the weight of his arm. I rest my forehead on the door. Don't cry, don't cry. I can't be in this room with Cooper. Ironic how this morning I would have been so excited to be in a room alone with Cooper. How quickly things can change. A guy I really liked thinks I'm not worth the trouble.

"Please let me go." My voice sounds so small.

"Let me explain." He's so close that I can feel his breath on my neck.

I turn around to face him. His chest is inches away from my face, and I see the worry etched on his face.

I duck under his arm, the one that was holding the door shut to create some distance, and turn to him, "It's fine, there's nothing to explain. I get it, I'm hard work. You don't want to deal with my problems, and why should you? We hardly know each other."

He shakes his head, "I admit, I freaked after I spoke to Harper. she said that you were fragile and...I don't know how to deal with someone fragile. What if I say the wrong thing? What if I hurt you?"

She said I was fragile. I'm not sure what upsets me more, that he can't be bothered because I'm high maintenance or that my best friend described me as fragile.

No one wants to be that. I hate that she thinks that about me.

I try to bite back tears. If my friend thinks that about me, what must everyone else think?

I smile at him, a small smile, still trying not to cry. "Don't worry about it. We need to do the music project together, let's just do that."

"Heidi, please let me talk to you properly. I can see you're upset now."

It escapes. I can't help it, there's nothing I can do. A tear rolls down my cheek. I'll never be good enough for anyone. This is my life.

"I need to go." My voice breaks as I say it and thankfully, he steps back from the door and lets me leave.

How am I going to get through the rest of the day, when all I want to do is get under my duvet and forget that the world exists?

Chapter Eleven

Cooper

I have hugely screwed this up. Well, Harper helped. Last time I trust her with anything. I shouldn't be mad at her though, Heidi is one of her best friends and she knew something was up. Still, Harper... thanks for nothing.

What move do I make now? I have no bloody idea. She likes music - maybe I could get her a present? A music-related one? What am I supposed to do, buy her a cd? Do they even sell those anymore? What about a music book? Maybe...

I didn't see her the rest of the day yesterday.

Alton towers is tomorrow, the entire school is going. The whole theme park hired out, it's cost thousands. Everyone has been talking about this trip, I can't let her go unhappy like this - especially when it's because of me. Ironic how she's unhappy because of me yet she is filling every bloody bit of room in my mind. She's in there. Whether I'm scared or not, she's there to stay.

After my shower, I get changed. Ed walks in as I'm towel drying my hair. He stares at me as he munches on a bag of m and m's. "What did you do?"

I sigh, "What do you know?"

"That you cocked up," he says in the middle of crunching.

"What, by talking to your girlfriend?"

He shakes his head. "Harper's always going to put her friends first. She's upset about it all. She said that Heidi was hurt because you were a no show, and she could read Harper like a book that she was hiding something and got it out of her. Don't blame her."

I shake my head. "I don't blame her, I knew it would be something like that. I hate that I've hurt someone's feelings. This is why I don't talk to people."

He seems as though he's battling with whatever he wants to say next but does anyway. "No one would blame you if you didn't want to go there with Heidi. This thing that's wrong with her, it would be hard to handle. She would be high maintenance, and you'd have to worry if you were going to upset her all the time."

It makes me angry that he talks like that about her, but why would he think anything else when I bailed on her?

It's too late for decisions as to whether or not to go for her. It's a yes. "It's not only the music thing, I... I like her."

"Well, yeah, of course you do."

My head snaps up to him. "What?"

"It's obvious you like her, she's the only girl that you've ever given the time of day to, even though half the girls in the school wouldn't say no. I mean, you've even got my half now as well, seeing as Harper has tied me down."

He's joking... I think.

"Well, if I did like her, if there was something, I've messed it up. If I helped her gain any confidence the other night, I completely stripped it yesterday. I was a coward."

"Like I say, I would get it."

"No, I'm not bothered, not really. I want to help her overcome it, but I was a coward because it's something I don't know anything about, and it scared me that I could say or do the wrong thing. That's why I asked Harper for help. I thought she could help me figure out how to act and stuff."

"Man, sounds like hard work to me. Surely if you have to be anything but yourself it's not worth it?"

"No, I don't mean be someone I'm not, I just want the facts before I dive in. But now I've screwed it up. There is no way she'd ever come near me again."

He shrugs, "You'll never find out if you don't try. Talk to her."

"I would if she would see me."

I get an idea. "Could Harper get her to come to hers?"

"Please leave Harper out of this."

I sigh, he's right. I nod, "I'll ring her, see if I can take her out for ice-cream or something."

"Don't lay it on too thick or she will go running, maybe keep liking her to yourself for a bit."

I laugh, "Don't worry, I wasn't going to mention that. I'm still getting my head around that myself."

He nods and pats me on the back, "Good luck, bro, we'll be in the den if you need us."

"K, and tell Harper I'm not mad at her, yeah?"

He nods, "Will do."

I sit on the bed and pick up my phone. Staring at it isn't going to make it work. I need to sort this out and the only way I can do this is face to face. I don't want to just turn up at her house - that would freak her out - but I do need to get her to agree to meet me.

I hit her number and it connects. Here we go. It rings for so long that I think she's not gonna answer. I check the time: 11 am. It's Saturday, maybe she's out and about somewhere.

I hear her voice, "Hello." Her voice sounds flat.

"Heidi, it's Cooper."

"I know."

"Yeah, er, I'm guessing you probably don't want to hear from me right now, but I was wondering if we could meet? Maybe take you for ice-cream or lunch or something? I need to talk to you about what happened, sort things out."

"You don't owe me an explanation, it's fine, let's leave it." She answers.

"No!" I answer a little too quickly and then say calmer, "I don't want to leave it, especially because when I explain things you won't hate me as much and feel bad about yourself like you are now."

I hear nothing but silence at the other end of the phone - does that mean she's thinking about it?

I push my luck. "Please?"

She sighs. "Fine, where do you want to meet?"

"I'll pick you up."

"No! I'll meet you there if you tell me where?"

Where can I say? I want to keep her there for a while so lunch would be good. "What about High Spot Deli?"

It's not too far, it's on the precinct and we can eat there.

"Yeah, I can't stay long though." Loosely translated, I don't want to spend too long in your company.

"No problem, is one okay? I'll buy you lunch."

"Yeah, whatever, see you there."

She hangs up. This won't be easy. I've got an hour, I start googling.

I walk inside the sandwich shop at ten to one. Getting there early means I'm fully prepared for when she arrives, which is a good job I did as it's crowded. I claim a table right in the corner with 2 seats and go to the counter to get us both a drink. I get her a Pepsi because that's what she got the other night at The Hideaway. If only I could rewind back to then.

The bell on the door rings and I turn around - it's her!

She's early; that's a good sign, surely?

I smile at her and she gives me a small smile in return. She's looks so pretty. She's wearing jeans with ankle boots and a long-sleeved purple top, it's oversized and has fallen off one shoulder, showing her bra strap. She looks incredible. She is beautiful. If I was the kind to use flowery words, I'd even say breath-taking. And doesn't have a clue that she is, which makes her even more so."

I point to the corner while I'm still in the queue, "I've got us a table."

She sees where I'm pointing and goes to sit.

When I take the drinks over, she's scrolling on her phone. She sees me. "Hey," she mumbles.

"Hi, thanks for coming. I got you a Pepsi, is that okay?"

She nods, "Sure."

"I thought I'd get us a drink and we can take our time deciding what to eat. You'll eat lunch with me, right?"

She glances around nervously, "Let's just get a drink for now, k?"

I decide to get right to it. "I'm sorry, Heidi...so sorry. I don't want you to think what I said had anything to do with you."

She shakes her head confused. No wonder. "You were talking about me."

"Well, yeah, I was, but it was more about me, my issues, than any issues you may have. It must have been awful overhearing that, but the truth is that Harper, and please don't be mad at her, but she freaked me out yesterday morning. I asked her about you, and she told me about your anxiety, which is fine, I knew about that anyway. But she said other stuff."

"What did she say?"

"She said that you were fragile and I of all people should be extra careful with your feelings."

She immediately blushes and stares at the table. Should I have told her that part? I figure the best thing is to be honest so that nothing can come out later. I'm in enough trouble here as it is.

"I'm not that fragile, it upsets me that she thinks of me like that." She plays with her bobbed hair and tucks it behind her ear. It kills me not to reach my hand up and do it for her. That would be overstepping right now.

"I'm sorry. It's because she cares about you. You know what she's like, if you're in her circle she cares about you fiercely, she's like a lion with cubs, and she was being protective over you. Don't be mad or upset at her for caring too much."

She shakes her head. "I can take care of myself."

"Of course, you can, but when you've got the support you take it, right?"

She shakes her head. "Do you understand that I don't want to be around you right now... or at all? You don't

113

want to deal with me. Why would I want to spend time with you? I nearly had a panic attack at the thought of meeting you today, so why on earth would I want to put myself through that? Do you have any idea what it's like to live your life like this? To always be in fear of something, trying not to think the worst of everything? I'm trying so hard to battle this everyday..." I swallow, my heart thumping so hard. I need to calm down.

I take a deep breath. "How do you think I feel that the one time I was proud of myself, and so pleased with how the week had gone, which was because of you, by the way, was the one time that I should have realised that I was out of my depth? So yeah, I was happy that I got on that stage - it took guts that people who don't suffer from anxiety would never understand. I pushed through and did it anyway and you seemed so happy for me. I thought you were on my side, had my back. All this has made me think is that people I presume I can trust, I can't, so I'm better being on my own."

"Jesus, Heidi, you don't need to feel like that. I was so happy for you that you got on stage and you're right, I have absolutely no idea what it's like to go through what you're going through, but I want to. I want to understand."

"Why do you care? Why are you here right now?"

She's shaking. What I say now will be the difference between her staying or leaving. I need to say something to change her opinion of me, and fast.

Chapter Twelve

Heidi

He stares at me after I've said it, but I need to know. Why is he bothering? Why is he staring at me like I'm crazy? I don't get why he is making all this effort when all we basically are, is work partners for the music show? I don't get it.

He clears his throat. "You're so talented, Heidi."

I study my hands. I find it hard to hear anything positive usually, but now? After all this, I can't see me believing it ever again.

I take a sip of my drink and put it back on the table. "Yeah, right."

He takes my hand that I've rested on the table and holds it flat in his hand. He turns it over, inspecting it. Every nerve in my hand goes hypersensitive, and it's as though I'm getting hundreds of tiny electric shocks, sending shivers throughout my body. What is he doing?

He bends my wrist and places my palm flat with his. I look up and he's staring at my hand as though it fascinates him.

"Um, Cooper, what are you doing?"

He glances at me and back to my hand. "Do you have any idea how talented you are, what amazing things you can do with these hands? This, right here, is an extremely special hand."

Ohh kayyy, so he's lost the plot.

"Cooper, you're being weird." I bend in to whisper.

He chuckles, "No, I'm not, just being honest. I listen to music, a lot of music, and you don't get how good you are. And Harper says you can sing too. I would love to hear that one day."

Don't hold your breath.

"Yeah, that's not going to happen." With how disappointed I am with him, I probably should remove my hand from his, but I can't. The way he's lightly touching it, revering it almost, I could let him do it all day.

Yup, let's do this for the rest of the day.

But of course, that would be weird. Something jolts through me as I see his eyes are on me.

"Can I have my hand back now?" I say with humour in my voice.

"I like you, Heidi."

Now my heart actually stops beating, at least for a second. Did he just say what I think he said? No, wait, he doesn't mean *like me* like me, he means I'm nice or whatever. Yeah, that'll be it.

"I'd like to say I like you too, but you're not my favourite person at the moment."

He shakes his head and clears his throat, "No, I mean, I *like you* like you."

My eyes go wide, and I push my glasses back up my nose, one of many nervous habits of mine.

He speaks again, probably getting nervous by my stunned silence.

"Don't panic, please don't panic and I would not say anything, but you're wondering why I'm showing so much interest. It doesn't take a genius to figure out I'm attract-ed to you."

"You're attracted to me?" I sound like I'm chewing a mouthful of biscuits. I need a drink, my mouth is so dry.

He nods. "I am."

"Why?"

He frowns, "Why not is a more apt question."

"No, it isn't. I don't know what to make of all this, I mean, I heard you say yesterday you want nothing to do with me."

"Heid, I don't understand about anxiety or panic at-tacks, I was ignorant and Harper scared me, I'm sorry. I know a little more now, I've been reading about it."

"You've been researching? Researching how to deal with me?"

He nods, "Don't be mad...only a little. This isn't easy for me, to say all this, put myself out there. I'm not expecting you to say anything now. I wanted to be honest. In fact, you can forget I said anything if it makes you feel any better."

"How am I supposed to forget that?"

He leans back in his chair. "What about you? Are you attracted to me at all?"

Oh no, hell no, no way I'm answering that. He doesn't need to know that I've crushed on him the last two years. I'm so conflicted right now because in one way I don't want to be near him after how he made me feel yesterday, but the other part of me, the part that was crushing on him for a long time, is doing cartwheels down the street that he's attracted to me.

I shake my head. "No way I'm answering that."

"Sorry, that wasn't fair. I didn't bring you here to tell you this - today isn't about me. I needed to explain about yesterday, how it was me, not you, that had the problem. Have I at least got that through to you?"

He likes me, he likes me, he likes me. Keep calm.

I nod, "Yeah, I guess. It hurt, though."

He seems sad that he hurt me. Maybe he did sound like he was a little scared and that's why I decide to give him the benefit of the doubt.

"Okay, fine, I won't hold that conversation against you."

He sighs. "Let's start with that. It's a win for me today. I didn't mean to put all that other stuff on you. I'm sorry. So, we can have lunch?"

I give a short nod. "We can, but can I ask one thing?"

"Sure."

"When you want to know anything about me, about what issues I have or anything, will you come to me? I won't bite. The more I worry about you talking about me behind my back, the more I'll close down."

His eyes go soft. "I can do that."

I smile, "Okay so let's have lunch."

I order a cheese and ham toastie and Cooper orders a meatball sub. It's the size of his arm and he eats it all, much to my amusement.

"So, Alton towers on Friday," he says through a mouthful. "You like rides?"

I wince, "I'm a bit of a wuss, no surprise there, so no not many rides, but I will give a couple of the medium ones a go, Sara and I said we will stick to the tea cups."

He smiles. "Will you have a spin with me?"

I tilt my head, "Maybe, we'll see."

His smile turns into a full-on grin. He really is so attractive, and he *likes me* likes me. I can't help but do a little dance inside.

"I'll talk you into it. What are you doing later? I'm going to the hideaway if you wanna come?"

I want to go but seeing as Mum and Dad think I'm with Harper right now, I can't stay out long. I shake my head, "Maybe next time, but I need to get back after this."

He nods, "I'm there tomorrow?"

"Again?"

He shrugs, "I like it there, it's nice to find a place with like-minded people. Plus, I can't play music at home. I mean, I can listen to music, but I can't play it. Also, Harper and Ed now they're together, Jesus, it's sickening."

I roll my eyes, "It is a bit, every time I turn around, they're kissing or gazing at each other."

He laughs, "You want to try living at my house? it's way worse than school." He wipes his mouth with the napkin.

"What did Edward mean? The other day, when he said that your Mum and Dad don't know what you're up to."

He sighs, "Story for another time."

"Oh sorry, I didn't mean to pry."

"No, it's fine, just..." he hesitates. "Don't say anything to anyone, yeah?"

I shake my head, "I won't."

"They have no idea how into music I am or that I want to pursue it as a career, they think it's a bit of fun."

Now I understand. "And you don't want to tell them."

He shakes his head, "It's a conversation I keep putting off, I mean, I'm doing A levels now, but I want to go into music production and writing after sixth form and I haven't told them yet. They keep asking, repeatedly, what I want to do, and I keep putting off that conversation. I'm not great with talking about deep stuff. I can't face it. I know I should, but that's what Ed was talking about. He knows that I've not been up front with them yet."

"What are your parents like? Will they be upset?"

He winces, "I'm not sure. They want us to learn a profession, it's up to us which, but they want us to have something we can rely on. They won't see me chasing my music dream as a profession."

"I bet if you don't put it off and talk to them you might be surprised." Again, I'm being a hypocrite when I'm hiding from my parenta who I'm actually with right now.

"I will, one day, when I have to. What about you, what do you want to do?"

I shake my head, "Not sure, something in music I hope." I fiddle with my empty plate and check the time. "I better go."

He nods, "I'll walk you home."

Oh god, how am I going to get out of this? I don't want to tell him that my dad doesn't want me to see him. "No, it's okay, I can walk on my own."

"No way, I'm walking you. I promise I won't try to hold your hand."

My heart flutters at the thought of walking with my hand in his. Urgh, I'm going to say no to that, I must be mad.

"If it's alright with you, I'd prefer to walk on my own, give me a chance to sort my head out."

He nods, "Oh okay, I guess. So, you wanna come to the club tomorrow?"

I want to, but where will I say I'm going? I could ask Harper to cover for me again... "Can I text you?"

He nods. "No problem, send me a text if you're going and I'll come and get you."

It would be better if I make my own way there, but I want to spend time with him and go to The Hideaway again, so I need to find a way to make it happen.

We say goodbye outside the cafe, and I turn to walk home. How the hell did I get myself into this? If my dad finds out that Cooper likes me, he definitely won't believe the party story. Oh my god, Cooper likes me likes me, I feel like I'm dreaming.

My phone rings in my pocket and when I check the display my stomach drops. Molly. My sister. She should be at Uni and never calls me. I look at Cooper. "I have to take this."

He nods and I click to answer. "Hey, sis."

"Hey Heidi, guess who's home?" she sings.

"Yey! You're home! How long for?"

"For the weekend, I wanted to surprise you all! There's a birthday party tonight that I wanted to come back for but today I'm all yours!"

"Oh great, well, I will be home soon."

"No problemo, Mum said you were at Harper's so we're on our way to pick you up - girlie shopping trip!"

Has it gotten hot? Suddenly everything looks blurred, and it takes all my will to hold on to the phone. This is my penance for telling lies, what the hell do I do now?

Chapter Thir~~

Heidi

"**N**o!" I snap. Cooper glances at me with a frown; he can obviously tell from my demeanour that something is wrong. I give a forced laugh, speaking into the phone. "Moll, give me a sec." I put the call on mute and turn to Cooper. "I should go, so I'll catch up with you tomorrow?"

Cooper raises his eyebrows at me. Damn, why does that look so good on him? Heidi, do not think about that right now, you need to get yourself out of this mess.

He answers, hesitantly. "Yeah, OK sure, speak to you tomorrow?"

I nod, giving him a smile and a little wave.

I hurry home. I have to make up something fast.

"I'm back. Harper and I came for lunch at High Spot but we're leaving now, Harper had to meet Ed." I cringe, more lies. "I'm on my way home."

OK, no problem, I'll make my way there and we'll pick you up on the way."

I sigh, relieved that I seem to have gotten away with it. Why do I feel like lying has just sent me down the rabbit hole and it's going to get worse and worse?

After shopping with Mum and Molly, we eat dinner. Later, I sink into a hot bath to try and relax me. It doesn't work. What can I do so sort this out? It was such a close call today; I could have gotten caught. I need to talk to someone. Harper will know what to do.

I stare at her name on my phone. Sod it, I'll call her.

She picks up, much to my relief.

"Hey, what ya doin?" she asks.

"Just having a bath, you got time to talk?"

"Yeah, just got back from the cinema, Ed and I are hanging out."

Crap, I can't talk to her in front of Ed.

"Oh right, you think maybe when you're on your own you can call me back?"

"It's OK, he's upstairs having a shower, I'm making us some supper. You can talk."

I relay to her what happened at the cafe and what my dad said about Cooper. She listens, making 'hmmm' noises and 'oh my gods' now and again, and when I finish, she sighs. "God, Heidi, this is a bit of a mess."

"I know, I know I should finish whatever the hell this is, or might be, with Cooper, but I like him - I've liked him for years, Harper."

"I know, and why should you have to? He's innocent, he did nothing wrong. Your dad is being so out of order."

"Yeah, and Mum is siding with him. What should I do?"

She's silent for a moment. "You know what we need to do? What would solve all this?"

Please have a plan, Harper. "What?"

"We need to find the guy that did this to you... or girl, it could have been anyone. If we did some detective work and found out, we could, I don't know, record them or something and then, bob's your uncle, problem solved. As long as they don't find out you've been going behind their back in the meantime."

I have to ask. "That's a great idea... apart from one thing...how the heck do we find out who did it?"

"Yeah, I don't know that part yet, but come on, whoever did it would have had booze on them, right? And they must have told someone."

I lean back in the bath, swishing the bubbles around my legs. "So many of them drink alcohol at those parties...god, their parents even give them a couple of bottles to take."

"Well, yeah, maybe a bottle of lager here and there or a Smirnoff Ice. But whoever spiked you, it must have been straight vodka or something to get you in that state. And you can't taste vodka like you can taste other alcohol so you wouldn't have been able to taste it in your coke much. Someone had a bottle of bloody vodka; you're not telling me no one saw that. We need to do some investigating.

We can come up with a plan of action and get the guys on the bus in on it."

She's starting to sound excited, and I don't know if that worries me or makes me feel better.

"I guess we can at least try. I feel so bad for Cooper, you know, helping me and getting all this."

"Yeah, me too, I know we always like to annoy each other but he's a good guy, he's like my brother. He's family, you know? Even though he's not."

"I get it. So yeah, let's do this. Let's clear his name." My mood lifts as I think about it. We can do this. Somehow. No idea how, but yeah, I feel hopeful.

"Can I ask you something though, Heidi?"

Uh oh. "Okay..."

"Why don't you tell Cooper about your dad?"

"Cos I don't want to make Cooper feel bad cos my dad is being horrible and I don't want him to never help someone if that situation arises again, God forbid." I answer. "But honestly? Mostly because I've crushed on him for two years and I don't want the chance to miss out on hanging out with him.

"It's so good spending time with him. He's nothing like I thought he was. He's sweet and funny and we get each other. I'm so excited about what could happen. What if he turned around and said it wasn't worth it? I mean, he hardly knows me."

"Blimey, you have it bad, don't you? I knew you liked him, but I think it's gotten to a whole new level." She pauses and then says, "Something tells me he wouldn't run. I've never seen him like this with a girl before."

Those butterflies wake up again; they're all ears for what Harper has to say.

I bite my lip. I love that she thinks that, but... "I don't know that for sure, so I don't want him to know. Okay? Just for now."

She sighs, "Fine, but I'm sure he'd be okay about it, he won't like you keeping this from him. He's upfront with people. Not always a good thing, but yeah, he's big on being honest."

"Well, it's not like he's my boyfriend or anything, we're doing a music project together. So, if we sort this out, he'll never find out will he? I want to see where this goes, if he might actually like me?"

She chuckles. "Oh, I'm pretty sure he likes you."

I hear a voice in the background, "Who is that?" I think it's Ed, but he and Cooper sound so alike.

"It's Heidi." She speaks into her phone, "Ed's back. Call you tomorrow to start our thing?"

I smile, she's so funny. She should have been in the Scooby Gang. She'd have made a perfect Daphne. "Yeah sure, thanks, Harper."

I take a while to get to sleep, tossing and turning before I do my sleep app then doze off. Today was stressful, but I got through it without a panic attack. Something I hadn't thought about until now. I actually did pretty amazingly today to keep my anxiety in check. Cooper likes me. I'm on cloud nine.

He's my first thought as soon as I wake up. He's admitted he likes me. Never in a million years did I think he would ever give me the time of day and here he is, saying he's attracted to me and asking if I'm attracted to him. Ha, what a joke. Er yeah, only me and every other girl in school. Well, us girls that are into the moody types anyway... which, apparently, I am.

He said he was going to The Hideaway today. I want to see him. I'm gonna do it. God, I want to have some fun. For as long I can remember I've lived in fear, second-guessing the things I do. Well he's been clear, he likes me. Harp and I started a plan to sort things out, but in the meantime, I want to spend time with the guy who likes me and that I've been crushing on for years. Is it too much to ask that I have some fun for once? And it's not like we're eloping, I'm meeting him to play and listen to music, that's it. I'm gonna do it.

I jump out of bed and try to decide what to wear. I'm guessing that he will only go in the afternoon, so I've got all morning to decide.

After lunch, after lying again to Mum and Dad and telling them I'm meeting friends, I stand in front of the doors to The Hideaway, trying to decide whether or not I have the guts to walk in.

My fingers do their usual tapping against my thighs as I try to calm myself with the rhythm of the imaginary guitar strings.

"Hey, good to see you again."

I spin around and Jen is walking towards me with a guy in tow, both pairs of eyes on me.

"Oh hey, I've come to see Cooper."

She nods and looks at the front door and back to me. "And the door is stopping you?"

I give a half-laugh, "Yeah, kind of. Actually it's my nerve, or lack of it, that's stopping me."

She gives me a knowing nod. "Ah, fair enough. Come in with us, safety in numbers and all that."

She links me and drags me with her, the choice is taken away from me.

I see him sitting at a table in the corner, he has earphones in, and his fingers are drumming on the table top while he writes something. He's dressed in jeans and a plain black t-shirt, as hot as ever. He is so deep in concentration that he doesn't even notice people have walked in.

Here goes. I walk over and sit beside him, causing him to startle.

He sees me and pulls his earphones out. "Heidi, what are you doing here?" he grins.

I give him a small smile, "You invited me, remember?"

He nods and closes the book he was writing in, smiling at me.

What do I do now? I didn't plan this far ahead.

Chapter Fourteen

Heidi

I have spent so much time wondering about what to wear and the fact that I want to do this, that I didn't think about what I was gonna do when I was here. I should have messaged him.

I wince, "Is it okay? That I turned up like this?"

"Hey, of course it is." He bites his lip. Oh my god, he needs to not bite his lip. "Me and the guys are about to practice though, let's get you a drink and, if it's you're happy to, maybe you can watch?"

I nod, relieved that he seems happy I came. "Sure, that sounds fun. What kind of music do you play?"

"Anything really, but we need a singer."

"Oh, how come?"

He shrugs, "The guitarist sings a little, but we need a female singer. They're difficult to come by."

I bite my lip. I can sing. Can I sing in front of a crowd... probably not, but maybe...? I mean, who would have thought I could play guitar on stage, and it's not as if there's an enormous crowd here right now. Even this time last week, I would have said no way. But now? The way he makes me feel, he's giving me so much confidence in myself. I feel like I can do anything. With nerves? Of course, yes, but I need to push myself.

"Um..."

"What?" he frowns at me. "You know someone?"

I shrug, "Kinda. I sing a little."

The shock on his face makes me laugh. "I know you can sing, but I didn't think for one second you would get on stage and do it."

"Well yeah, I don't do it in front of people though, not usually, but I seem into trying new things at the moment, right?"

"Is there anything you can't do?"

See? It's him saying things like that to me that makes me believe I can do it.

I roll my eyes, "Yeah, it's everything else I struggle with, the normal day-to-day stuff that people take for granted."

"Sorry, yeah. So how good are you?"

"I can carry a tune."

"You're good."

I shrug but say nothing.

"You should sing with us today."

I nod. "I'll see what you're singing first, if it passes my quality test then sure."

"Ah, cocky about your musical tastes. Don't worry, you won't be disappointed. Plus, we have so much material we will find something that suits your voice. If you had to compare yourself to someone, who would you say?"

"Oh no, no way I'm saying that. You can see when I sing and decide for yourself."

"You amaze me every day, Heidi. I wish you knew how special you are."

I grin, happy at the thought of pleasing him. Hopefully, I won't choke up.

Come on Heidi, you've got this.

I can feel it inside me, threatening to take over. The panic; the dry mouth, heart beating faster and harder than usual, feeling as though its in the back of my throat. The fight and flight wanting flight so bad. But no. It's not beating me forever. This time, I choose fight.

I step up to the mic and feel the buzzing of the electricity coming from it as I gently place my hand around it.

I close my eyes, waiting for the click of Cooper's drumsticks, counting us in for the beginning of the song.

The chords of Brandi Carli's 'The Joke' start to play. It was a song I suggested and luckily, they knew the song because it had recently gone viral on Tiktok.

I sing the first note and the nerves float away. I forget I'm singing in front of people, my eyes closed, feeling every single word of this beautiful song. Every word of it meaning something to me.

What I don't realise as I'm singing is that everyone in the room stops what they're doing, and the atmosphere of the whole room changes. I lose myself in the song, the melody and sing my heart out.

When I sing the final note, I look around the room and realise that people are watching me as they burst into whoops, cheers and whistles.

I dip my head in embarrassment but inside I'm screaming. I bloody nailed that and loved every minute. My grin might not be visible on the outside but it's consuming me on the inside. I did it.

I feel movement behind me and turn around. He's right there, starting at me. He makes a sound like a half-huff, half-laugh and then just shakes his head.

"I can't...I don't..." he breaks off.

What is he trying to say? I mean, I *thought* it was good, was everyone else hearing something else? But the clapping... unless... were they clapping because they're glad it ended?

I wait for him to carry on then lose patience.

"You didn't like it?" I ask.

His head jerks back in shock. "You're kidding right?"

I shake my head slowly.

"Heidi, Jesus Christ, your voice. It is *unbelievable*. You are scary talented, you know that right?"

My shoulders relax, I hadn't realised I was holding my body stiff, waiting for his reaction. He liked it.

I smile, shyly. "I have to be good at something, right?"

He laughs and shakes his head. "Well, you sure as hell are good at that!"

He stares at me then says in a low tone, so that only I can here. "Where have you been?"

I'm not sure how he wants me to answer that - but the tone he used, I feel it in my belly. I love that I impressed him.

Jay, the bass player, walks over and throws his arm around Cooper. "Dude, I think we found our new band member."

My eyes widen and I stare at him. "*What?*"

"You *have* to be our new singer. You just have to be. Right, guys?" he says, looking around at the others.

Cooper leans in, "I don't think they're gonna take no for an answer." He gives me a lopsided grin.

They want me in their band! Me! Shy me!

I mean, they don't perform anywhere, so that makes it a little easier for me to agree but still. I am actually a rock chick!

I let out a laugh, "I guess I'm in the band then."

I'm gonna need some time to get my head around this – hmm around three years should do it!

When it gets to four-ish, I need to head back. I told mum I'd be back at five.

"I should get going."

137

"I'll walk you home."

I shake my head, "It's fine, I can walk home, you stay here with your friends."

"Well, what if I don't want to stay here with my friends, what if I want to walk my girl home?"

Did he just say...?

"Your girl?" I croak.

He looks at the floor and when he glances back at me it seems as though... it seems as though he's blushing! "Well, yeah, hopefully, soon. I can hope."

His eyes hold mine for what feels like an hour but is actually only a few seconds more than normal. Something runs through me, warmth, excitement, hope. Hope for what Cooper and I could have between us.

I'm not going to say no to that, am I?

"Okay, you can walk me home."

I can talk him into walking me part way when we get there, but right now I don't want to leave him, I want to spend all the time I can with him, so I'll take it.

He grins. "I'll say bye to the guys."

I nod and turn and wave at the guys on the stage and one of them speaks into the mic, "bye, new band member."

I laugh and give a little wave as I walk towards the door, saying bye to Jen and the other girls as I leave.

I wait outside for him to join me and breathe in the exhilaration of what it feels like when things go right, everything goes according to plan. Today has been the best. Has anything ever felt as good as today feels? Sure, that I lied to be here doesn't sit quite right with me, but the outcome way outweighs the fact that I had to tell a little white lie to be here.

The door opens and my heart rate quickens as I see him walking toward me. He is so handsome, so everything, and for some reason, he seems to think I'm worth his time. I want him to kiss me. Maybe I should give him a sign that I'm okay for him to do that, or am I moving way too fast? My heart has been there for two years though, so I want to embrace all the emotion all at once.

We walk towards home, and I feel the warmth of his hand as he slides it into mine, our fingers entwining. At his touch, my whole body hums.

"Is this okay?" He lifts both our hands in question.

I nod, "Yeah, it's nice. I like it."

He drops our hands and nudges my shoulder a little. "Me too."

I motion towards the park that I walked through earlier. "Want to walk through the park?"

He nods and we veer off in that direction. It's cold now and the park is deserted. This would be the perfect spot for a kiss.

He walks over to a nearby large round netted swing and perches on the edge. He grins, "Sit on here with me for a while."

I should get back, but five minutes won't hurt, I don't want to pass this opportunity up.

I take him in, sitting there.... I should kiss him. That would show him how much I like him. Crap, how do I do it? Harper said to wing it when we talked about first kisses, she said it comes naturally. Here's hoping. Don't overthink this Heidi, just do it.

I lunge over to him and just have time to see his startled expression before my lips land on his. Totally taken by surprise, he makes a grunting sound and kind of falls backwards and I tumble on top of him, the weight of me winding him. He makes an oof sound. Well, I've either winded him or my knee has gone in a place that no knee should go.

Total disaster...buildings falling to the ground, tsunamis kind of disaster.

There is no way out of this that isn't mortifying. So, I sit and kind of roll off him and fall to the side. We must be a right sight.

I glance at him, horrified, what is going on in his head? A few seconds later that question is answered when he throws his head back and bursts out laughing. Oh my god, the shame. He now thinks I'm hilarious. Jesus, what did I just do? "I'm sorry, that wasn't... that didn't go as I planned."

He raises an eyebrow while still laughing, "You reckon? Thank God that wasn't what you'd planned."

I shake my head and try to find the humour, chuckling with him. I hide my head in my hands, we're both still lying on the swing.

I mumble. "That is the most embarrassing moment of my life, and this is coming from someone that was falling down drunk in front of all her school friends a couple of weeks ago."

I can tell he is trying to compose himself. That's right, I'm a walking mistake.

He finally stops laughing. "I'm sorry, you took me by surprise, that's all. I didn't even realise a kiss was on the table, the next minute you're coming at me. If I'd have known your intention..."

"Don't, please stop talking."

"I'm sorry. Let's have a do-over."

"What, no, never!" I will never mortify myself like that again.

"Never?" his voice dips low.

"Well, maybe not never, but I can tell you I won't be the one to instigate it if there is a next time."

"But if I instigate it there may be a next time?" his voice has gone husky.

My heart skips a beat. He wants there to be a next kiss. He must have a death wish, but he wants a do-over, that's the main thing. Those dark brown eyes watching me, waiting for an answer, easy decision. "Maybe."

"Okay." He says softly, reaching towards me. I wonder what he's doing but then he does something that takes my breath away. He tucks a strand of her hair behind my ear. His fingers touch the side of my face, lingering on there with a feather touch.

I don't deserve for him to be so nice to me, so gentle.

He leans towards me and his lips brush my cheek in a barely-there gesture. He leans back and jumps off the swing, holding my hand to help me get out. "Come on, let's get you home."

Chapter Fifteen

Cooper

I reach over and grab her hand. How I wangled sitting next to her on the coach on the way home is anyone's guess. Guess the teachers were in a good mood. But here I am, after getting to spend most of the day with her, and she is resting her head on my shoulder while fighting to stay awake.

"You had a good day, Heid?"

She nods. "It's been great." She lets out an enormous yawn, "I'm so exhausted now, do you mind me resting my head on you?"

I kiss the top of her head. "No, I don't," I say quietly and put my arm around her shoulders, drawing her into me. I could happily sit like this all night.

I breathe in the scent of her hair; it smells fruity, possibly mango or something. It's nice, it's her.

It's been a good week. We've got on at school, worked on the play together and she's been to The Hideaway. There's just something... something holding her back from me that I can't fathom. I will get there with her though, her anxiety has been so much better and she doesn't seem shy anymore when she's talking to me like she used to, so that's a win.

I lay my head back in the seat and close my eyes. She takes a deep breath and snuggles into me further. This is fast becoming something I can't control. She is taking over my every thought. We click, we can literally talk forever about music, and we have nearly finished writing the song. She played for me in the music room and I am mesmerised watching her. She loses herself in that guitar and I'm privileged that she lets me hear her play and her voice, oh my god, I could listen to her sing every word for the rest of my life and still not get tired of it.

I want to kiss her. I want to kiss her so bad it's killing me. I've had some chances, but after last week's fiasco, I want it to be right, be perfect. Seeing as, well if we're not counting last Sunday, which we're not, it's my first kiss. Never really had an interest to have a girlfriend before now. Always felt like they're not worth the trouble, but she came along, and she's worth every bit of trouble.

Tonight. I'm going to kiss her tonight. I'm not waiting any longer.

I should have the opportunity tonight. She's sleeping over at Harper's, so she's coming home with us. Harper's mum works nights, so Heidi is keeping her company, which means that I get to spend the evening with her. The plan is to watch a movie at Harpers and order pizza. Mum and dad will no doubt keep bobbing in to check we're behaving ourselves, but yeah, the four of us have the house to ourselves. If ever there was a perfect opportunity, it's tonight. And if no opportunity arises, I'm going to make sure I create one.

She stirs when we're arriving at Arrowsmith and sits up, confused, sleepy and so damn cute.

She straightens her glasses. "Hey, where are we?"

"We are at school, and I would like to take this opportunity to thank you for the scintillating conversation you have provided me with on the way home. I have been so entertained."

"Talk in my sleep, do I?"

I chuckle, "No, but you do snore."

Her eyes widen, "I do not."

I shake my head, and look at her softly, "No, you don't. Come on, get your coat on and your things together, we can get off in a minute."

"I'm sorry, I can't believe I slept the whole way."

"It's fine, I enjoyed having you lean on me." I lean in to mumble to her and watch her cheeks go pink. She blushes so easily, I love it. In fact, I try to make her blush at least once a day. Cruel? Oh yes, but I can't help it, what can I say? I have a cruel side.

She stands and gets her things together as I sit and watch her flapping around all half asleep. So cute.

We order pizza when we get to Harper's - we're all starving, her mum is leaving for work shortly and gives us a list of dos and don'ts, explaining that she's trusting us and my parents will pop in - at any given time. We all roll our eyes; we understand the terms and conditions and will be on our best behaviour. I'm just happy I get to spend the evening with her.

"What film should we watch, Heidi?" Harper asks.

Heidi taps her fingers on her mouth. She is so cute. "Not sure, maybe an action film?"

Harper rolls her eyes, "Why action?"

"Well, it's not fair to make the guys watch a girlie film." She sighs. "What about a comedy?"

"Whatever, I don't mind what we watch. Have a search on Netflix."

I watch the exchange between them, not giving a damn what we watch as long as I get to sit next to her while we watch it. Harper turns to Ed, "Want to come in the kitchen to sort out plates and drinks and things, ready for the pizza?"

Edward smiles at Harper and agrees rather too quickly to be the host. Yeah right, of course they're sorting out plates.

I turn to Heidi who is standing at the TV scrolling through Amazon Prime. I stand behind her and put my hand on her hip, making her jump. "See anything you like?" I say into her ear, loving that I make her shiver.

Her eyes meet mine, it's clear that she has seen something she likes. She clears her throat "Er yeah, maybe this?"

She points to the TV, Uncharted is highlighted. "Yeah sure, looks good."

I can't wait any longer. "Heidi?"

"Yeah?"

"I want that do over now." My voice is husky.

Her eyes go wide and she scans around the room. "Here?"

I nod slowly but don't say anything.

"But Ed and Harper could walk in at any time."

I smirk, "They're busy."

Her eyes soften and fall to my mouth. "You want to kiss me now?" she whispers.

I nod, "I do, come here."

I put my other hand on her hip and pull her into me, so our faces are an inch apart. She is so beautiful. I lift my hand to cup her cheek and she closes her eyes slowly, nestling her face into my hand.

"I've been waiting to do this all week, see what those lips feel like, taste like."

Her eyes open and there is no mistaking she wants that too. I lower my head to hers...

"We're back."

Harper's voice behind me. Could her timing be any worse? I mean, they're constantly kissing in front of everyone, they get a chance to be alone and they're back that quick? For god's sake.

"Oh!" Heidi pulls away from me, her eyes wide.

"Any chance you'll go back into the kitchen?" My eyes are on Heidi when I say it, but we all get that it's directed to Harper.

"No, sorry, pizza's here. You didn't hear the door?"

I drop my hand from Heidi and take a step back, giving her a rueful smile.

"Obviously not."

Heidi glances over my shoulder at Harper, who is obviously doing something behind my back because Heidi chuckles.

I wink at her and turn to Harper. "Come on, let's eat."

We eat while watching the movie. I should be engrossed in the story line but all I can think of is how close I got to kissing her and how much I want to kiss her again. I need to get her alone. Jeez, anyone would think that Harper and Edward are the chaperones. Mum came in to check on us half an hour ago and we were all behaving ourselves so they were happy with the warning that they will come again in another hour or so.

Right, that's it, I'm getting her in the kitchen, alone. Now.

Chapter Sixteen

Heidi

I'm sitting here staring at the screen, trying not to touch my cheek where it's still tingling from his touch earlier. He was actually going to kiss me. I've been waiting all week for him to try again. I promised myself I wouldn't instigate it, so I've been waiting around and he springs it on me when I least expect it. Oh, and great timing, Harper.

I'm so conscious of the fact that his knee is two inches from mine and keeps brushing against me accidentally. Is it accidentally, or is he trying to torment me on purpose?

I stare at the screen, trying to remember what the heck this film is about. I love Tom Holland, and I've been waiting to watch this, but I can't concentrate right now. Every inch of my skin is buzzing with excitement at the thought of what is coming, I've never kissed anyone before – we won't talk about last week's disaster – but what if he's kissed tonnes of girls and has lots of experience? What if I'm a terrible kisser?

He breaks me out of m' internal ramblings when he stands quickly.

"Gonna get more drinks and the nibbles." He turns to me. "You coming to help?"

His face is serious. Is something wrong?

I nod slightly, "Yeah, sure." He turns around and walks out as Ed shouts, "Bring the minstrels will you."

I follow behind him to the kitchen. Once inside, he reaches behind me to close the door.

"What's up?" I ask, wondering what this change in mood is about.

"Nothing, well yeah, something."

He steps into me and the look in his eyes is so intense, my insides are turning to liquid. All my body goes hot. This is it, he's going to kiss me.

I hold up my hand. "Wait!"

He stops his advance and frowns.

"I need to tell you something," I blurt out.

"You don't fancy me."

My mouth drops open and his eyes go to it. "Er, no, not that."

His eyes go back to mine. "So, you *do* fancy me," he breathes.

I nod, "Yeah, definitely."

"So, what's the problem?"

I lean into him and whisper, "I can't kiss."

He bites his lip and tilts his head to the side. "Really? Let's see about that."

My breathing becomes erratic as he steps into me, his body flush with mine. God, I want to kiss him, I don't want to be bad, but I need to see what it's like to kiss Cooper. My head has been full of thoughts of kissing Cooper.

He places his hand on my neck, his thumb stroking my jawline. How does he do that so softly?

His head bends towards me and his mouth is on mine. Those lips that I've been dreaming about. This isn't like last time, this is serious, he means business and sod it, so do I.

I press my lips into his, parting them a little and reach my hand to rest on his neck, touching his soft hair.

He parts his lips and inhales as he deepens the kiss, and we revel in the sensation of our mouths moving together in unison, perfectly, I had nothing to worry about. I'm a natural at this kissing lark after all. In fact, I want to do it all god damn night.

He breaks off and moves his mouth along my jaw line, down to my neck, giving me open-mouthed kisses there. I close my eyes, revelling in the sensation of being drawn into heaven and hell all at the same time. It feels so right for him to be kissing me.

A sigh escapes me and his lips trail back up my neck and back to my mouth. His hands slide down my arms and around my waist, flattening his palms on my back he pulls me into him even further. I like kissing. I like it a lot!

He breaks off from the kiss, his chest moving up and down rapidly, his breathing fast.

"God Heidi, that was, that…" his eyes are so dark with intensity, he can read me like a book. No point in hiding anything.

My breathing is matching his and we are still locked in each other's arms. "That was good."

He gives a half-laugh, "yeah."

"Suppose you better let me go now, otherwise we'll be in here all night."

"Yeah." He sighs, but he doesn't let me go, he stares at me.

"Cooper?"

"I don't want to."

I lift my hand and my fingers trace his eyebrow and he closes his eyes.

We hear Edward shouting from the living room. "Guys, whatever you're doing in there can't be as important as my minstrels. Hurry up, would you?"

I smile at him, "Come on."

He steps away from me and immediately it feels chilly. He spins, grabs the bag of minstrels, muttering, "I'm gonna throw them at him in a minute," and he storms out.

Oh dear.

I walk over to the worktop to put some of the other snacks into bowls. I hear him walk back in, so I ask. "Do you want to do the drinks?"

He sighs and grabs the coke and Fanta. "Whatever."

I turn to him. He looks miserable, but not as miserable that I am now that it's over. I hate Edward right now and his chocolate addiction. "You sulking now?"

"I don't sulk. It's him, he drives me crazy."

"You drive me crazy."

Oh my god, did I just say that?

"Christ." e mutters.

He grabs a bowl out of my hand and grabs my waist, in a flash, he lifts me so that my bum hits the counter. He steps into my legs. Such an intimate move and so unexpected.

"Wow, what are you doing?" I sound like I've run a marathon.

He grins, "Waiting for you to kiss me."

He thinks I'm going to put up with a fight about that? Now I've actually experienced kissing him, I won't be passing up an opportunity. It's now the joint first place of my favourite pass times, along with playing the guitar.

I rest my hands on his neck and bend my head towards his, his mouth meeting mine halfway. We kiss and kiss for quite a while. Harper and Edward will one hundred per cent know what we're up to, but we don't care, we are having way too much fun. Just being able to kiss him like this after all this time and all these times I've imagined what it would be like, well I ain't stopping now.

Our mouths meld, our tongues touch and it's electrifying. Unfortunately, so entrancing that we don't hear the door.

What we do hear is someone clear their throat loudly, making us jump apart.

A man is standing there, with a smirk on his face and his arms folded staring at us. He obviously walked in through the back door. He has a resemblance to Ed and Cooper. It's got to be their dad, who appears as though he can't decide whether to be amused or mad.

Heat rushes to my face. I have never been so mortified in all my life; the lunge kiss was bad, but this? This is so terrible. This is how I wanted to meet Cooper's dad for the first time? Right in the middle of a make-out session?

"Dad! Shit," Cooper says, half laughing.

"Language, Cooper. I see I'm interrupting."

I jump off the worktop as Harper and Edward walk in. Great, more mortification.

"Hey Dad, what s up?" Ed asks. "Time to check on us again?"

He glances at Edward and back to Cooper, "Yeah, good job I did I reckon, told your Mum she was being daft getting me to check on you, but with how engrossed these two were with each other when I walked in, reckon she was on point."

Ed and Harper both laugh. Of course, it was us that got caught and not them.

"Dad, leave it," Cooper says, now all business.

He turns and grabs my hand, pulling me to his side. "Dad, this is Heidi."

"Yeah, I figured. Nice to meet you, Heidi."

My heart is hammering. What is he going to think of me? I swallow, I need to speak or he's going to think I'm weird or worse, rude. I open my mouth to speak but nothing comes out and silence stretches before us all. I see Cooper watch me from the side but I'm frozen to the spot. This is not me, being caught making out with someone in the kitchen by their parents for goodness' sake. The familiar feeling of an upcoming panic attack starts to build and my breath starts to get shallow.

I need to get control. Cooper squeezes my hand and I look at him. He's watching me, with a frown on his face. Oh god, they're watching me. I need to get out of here.

"Nice to meet you, sir, I'm sorry, I have to go," I croak out and pull my hand from Cooper's, before fleeing upstairs to the bathroom, closing the door behind me. Well, if there was a way to make a bad impression on a parent, I have mastered it.

I sit on the toilet with the lid down and put my head in my hands. Get a grip, you can do this. I want to go home. No! You know what this is, and you know you can get a handle on it. Breathe.

There's a knock at the bathroom door, "You okay?" It's Harper.

"Yeah, just the usual, I'll be out in a minute," I croak out.

She understands, "I'll get rid of Cooper's dad, okay? You won't have to face him."

I groan. This is awful. "Thanks."

I give myself five minutes to get myself together. I never get in trouble, I never do anything like this, and now what? I'm lying to my parents, smooching guys in kitchens, what am I doing?

I need to go home and get my head straight.

When I walk into the kitchen, Edward and Cooper are there, whispering, their eyes following me when I walk in.

I look at Cooper, "I want to go home."

His eyes go wide and he shakes his head. "Don't worry, Dad is cool."

I shake my head and fold my arms across my body, "I've made a fool of myself. I'm embarrassed and I want to go home." I'm going to cry.

Ed steps forward, "Come on, Heid, so what? You two got caught so you were too embarrassed to speak to Dad. It's no biggie, he will see the funny side of it."

I shake my head, "I never want to see him again, I'm so embarrassed."

"Heidi...please, let's talk," Cooper pleads.

"I can't explain it, I need to go home, right now."

He sighs and pushes himself off the counter. "Okay, let's get your things." Disappointment in his voice. I get it, I'm disappointed with myself too.

My heart is heavy as I watch him go around and collect my things. Harper stands and grabs my arm. She pulls me up the stairs and into her bedroom.

"Guys, give us a minute," she yells behind her.

She shuts her bedroom door once we're inside. "Breathe, Heidi. You don't need to go home. You're panicking and it's taking over. Close your eyes, in through your nose, out through your mouth, slowly, feel the breath going in and going out. Just like you told me.

I do as she says and close my eyes, drawing the breath into my body and breathing out again. I clear my mind of anything else and concentrate on my breath. I do it a few times and the panic starts to subside. We're quiet for a while, then I sit on the bed, opening my eyes.

"I'm okay," I mumble.

She nods and smiles. "Staying?"

What should I do? The panic takes over and makes the body go into fight or flight, but with panic, it's always flight. When I can get the panic to subside, the rational side of me lets me decide on fight or flight, instead of going straight to flight. I don't want to go home, if I do, it will be so much harder to face everyone next time. If I stay, we can laugh it off and get on with our night, and it won't make that amazing kiss a big mistake. I have to stay.

"If I don't die from embarrassment, yes."

"Want me to get Cooper to come up?"

My eyes widen, "To your bedroom? No!"

"To talk, clear the air."

"I suppose. God, I bet he wants to run home and pretend he never met me."

"Hey, don't talk like that. You think any of us are perfect? We're not. You're not. Get over it, he doesn't think anything, he's worried about you, okay?"

I nod and she leaves. I carry on with my breathing exercise, trying not to let all the other thoughts in, just concentrate on keeping calm and having to talk to Cooper.

There's a little knock at the door and he walks in.

"Hey," he whispers.

"I'm sorry I freaked."

He shakes his head and comes and sits on the bed at the side of me. "It's fine, don't worry."

"I'm so embarrassed."

"Hey, it' doesn't matter, forget about it."

"But your dad..."

"Don't worry. If it's okay with you, I'll explain what happens to you sometimes and he'll be good. He thought it was hilarious catching us, I mean, Mum would have been a different story, but Dad is cool."

He has his hands clasped together on his knee, unsure of what to say. He's probably scared I'm gonna go off on one again.

"Why are you being like this with me?"

His head snaps up, he's frowning. "Like what?"

"Nice, giving me your time, your attention. You must see now, it's more trouble than it's worth, that I'm more trouble than I'm worth."

"Don't say that, ever. Your anxiety doesn't define you. You had a panic attack, so what? You think none of us have our issues? Because believe me, we do. I hate being around people. I would rather be alone in my bedroom than anywhere else, talking to people. I hang out at Hide-away because everyone is like that there, but I don't like humans much at all. So does that mean that I'm not worth the effort too?"

I shake my head. "Of course not."

He shrugs, "I don't like you putting yourself down. You are amazing in so many ways, Heidi, but you have this little thing, these panic episodes, which alright, isn't little to you, so I shouldn't describe it like that, but you think it takes over all the good stuff." He shakes his head and sighs. "The good stuff is all I see and I see your anxiety as this small part of you. It's not you. It doesn't have to control you, right? I mean, I'm only learning about this stuff, but you controlled it."

"Well, yeah, with Harper's help."

"So what? You needed help, you have people around you that will help, so you're good. You've got this."

"You're amazing," I blurt out. He really is, talk about saying all the right things, making me feel special, I've almost forgotten the mortifying scene downstairs.

His eyes soften and his shoulders relax. "Well, now you're seeing straight. Come on, let's go watch the film yeah?"

I stand, "Thanks, Cooper."

He leans in and kisses me on the cheek. "Anytime."

We all have our flaws. I'm trying to be what everyone wants all the time when I should just be me - flaws and all. Words are easy, thoughts are easy. Carrying these thoughts through into actions is the hard part. But I need to learn, or I'm going to let life pass me by.

Sometimes it's harder to make the right choice when I can be living in my comfort blanket.

Chapter Seventeen

Heidi

Four days later, it's practice day.

We have finished writing the song, we just have to put it to Mr Bell to see if he likes it plus, we have put the show together in an order that works, so we have to run through the practice.

Cooper and I have spent a lot of time together this week. All the time we could. Harper and I have a super-plan in place to find out who spiked me. So far, we have come up with nothing but Harper is confident that we will find out who it was - a lot more confident than I am.

The bell has gone for the end of class, so I make my way across the yard to the music block.

"Heidi!" I hear my name, but I don't see anyone.

I turn back and walk towards the block when I hear it again when I see Ethan running towards me. Oh god, what does he want? Just because I can talk to Cooper these days, doesn't mean I'm any better when it comes to strange guys.

"Oh hey, Ethan," I say, looking around as though searching for an escape route.

"Hey, I've been wanting to talk to you, got a minute?" he adjusts his backpack.

I shake my head, "No, I'm in a hurry, I have practice after school." And I want to be anywhere but here.

"Oh, I'll walk you there."

Oh no, why? I don't want him to!

"Er, okay. What's up?"

Read the room, Ethan, I don't want to talk to you.

"I wondered if you wanted to go to Connor's party with me at the weekend?"

Why would he want me to do that?

"Um, why?"

He laughs, "Why do you think? I want to spend time with you, get to know you better."

I stare at the floor as I walk. "No, but thanks for asking."

"Come on, it'll be fun." He stops walking and grabs my arm, so I stop.

I tense up. "I'm sorry, no, I don't want to."

"Come on, it'll be fun and you'll lighten up once we're there."

"Lighten up?" something in his tone makes me stop in my tracks.

"Yeah, like you did the other week."

162

My face gets hot. Why is he bringing that up now?

I'm not sure what to say and breathe a sigh of relief when I see Cooper jogging toward me.

"Hey." He comes to a stop when he sees us and glances between us both, frowning at Ethan. "What's going on?"

Ethan shrugs, "Nothing, I'm asking Heidi if she wants to come to the party with me at the weekend."

Cooper's eyebrows disappear into his hairline. "I see, so I guess she's just in the middle of telling you she has a boyfriend."

Ethan glances at me and back to Cooper. "You?"

Cooper nods, "Yeah, me. She won't be going to any party with you."

They glare at each other for a few seconds before Ethan says, "Fair enough, see you in class, Heidi." And walks away.

Cooper asks, "Who the hell is that?"

My mouth must be open because I'm still gob-smacked that he said he was my boyfriend. Cooper is my boyfriend? We hadn't talked about that, we've just been hanging out. He probably said it to get rid of Ethan.

"Um, he's in my English class."

"I don't like the way he was looking at you."

"He wasn't looking at me funny."

"Yeah, he was."

I shake my head, "He wasn't looking at me in any way."

He doesn't answer me, instead he just bites his lip, staring at me.

"What? "I ask.

He frowns. "Have you ever had any issues with him, or has he ever paid you any special attention?" he asks, his eyes studying me.

I shake my head, then remember something, "Well, he asked if we could meet up the other week, but that was because we got an English project together."

"Yeah, right, he probably couldn't believe his luck he got paired with you. Was he at George's party?"

My eyes widen, "I know what you're thinking, but you're overreacting."

He looks in the distance where Ethan has run off, "Am I? We'll see."

In practice, we go through the whole show. The performance is in a week, and we need to get organised. There are extra meet ups after school every day this week and some lunches, so I get to spend a huge amount of time with Cooper.

"Okay, that's enough for now," Mr Bell says, and a sigh of relief goes around the room. Preparing a show is stressful and he has worked us hard.

"Heidi and Cooper, Annabel and Ben, can you guys stay behind for an extra ten minutes?"

I look at Cooper, puzzled. Annabel is a singer and Ben plays the keyboard.

When the room has emptied, he turns to us. "Hear me out - the more I think about it the more I think about how amazing this would be." He pauses for dramatic effect. "You guys would make an amazing band."

I take a sharp breath in. How can he ask me this? I just want to work behind the scenes. I've started performing a little at Hideaway, but this is a whole new ball game. He's asking me to perform in front of a school full of kids.

His eyes fall on me. "All these three need you, Heidi. They need a guitarist. I get that you don't want to play in front of anyone, but Jesus you are so good, you could do it with your eyes closed. And how amazing would it be if you four came together?"

We all check each other out. Annabel is in sixth form, the year above Cooper so I've not really spoken to her, and Ben is in the year below me.

Anabel speaks, "I guess we could give it a go?"

Time to speak before they get their hopes up. "I don't perform in front of people." But that's not strictly true anymore. Cooper's eyes are on me. The more time I've been spending with Cooper the more I've been performing, but there was no audience. Sometimes there have been a few people there, some watch and I've been okay, but as Coop says, they're like-minded people, introverts like me. But still, I have been doing something I never thought I'd have the guts to do. So maybe, just maybe, I could do this?

I sense Cooper watching me. I can tell he wants me to do this. I don't want to let him down, but more importantly, I don't want to let myself down. Am I going to live like this forever? I don't have to sing at school, I'll be on stage with three other people and I'm confident playing, I have the knowledge. I might regret this, but...

"Okay, I will give it a go."

"Really?" Cooper asks.

I smile, "Yeah, why not?"

He looks at me softly. "Yeah, why not." When he gives me that look, coming from him when his usual expression is so stern, I swear all logical thought goes out of the window.

"Excellent!" Mr Bell booms. "Got time to get up there and have a go now?"

I nod and we all agree and get back on the stage.

Cooper, because he's on drums, leads. Mr Bell wants us to try Counting Stars, One Republic and we smash it. We all gel amazingly and Annabel's voice is gorgeous and is perfect for the song.

When we all play the final chords, we look around each other and grin. That worked.

Ben speaks, "That was awesome. We should start a band for real!"

Two band offers in one week. What is going on?

We all laugh at ben, but it was crazy how well we played together for the first time. A bubble of excitement starts inside me that when I play in front of an audience next week, we're actually gonna be good, people are gonna like what they hear, and I get a buzz at the thought.

We pack our things and Cooper comes over. "Take you home?"

I nod. I'll get him to drop me off at the shop again.

Once we're in the car and he's driving he says. "So... you and Harper have a plan to find the guy that spiked you?"

My back straightens. I hope Harper hasn't told him everything, I don't want him to know the why.

"Um yeah, why?"

He shakes his head. "No reason, I was wondering if you'd gotten anywhere?"

I think back to my earlier conversation with Ethan. "No, not really."

"What have you done so far?"

"Harper has asked around the guys that were there, casually, seeing if anyone was drinking. Trouble is, a few of the guys were."

"What about that guy before? He was into you, Heidi."

I shiver a little at the thought. I don't like Ethan. I'm not sure about him. I might try to find out a little about him.

"Leave it with me, I can think of a way," Cooper says.

"I don't want you getting in any trouble."

"Trouble how?" he glances at me and then faces back to the road.

"Well, whoever did that to me can't be very nice, and I don't want you crossing anyone and ending up in a fight or something."

He scoffs. "I don't care about that. Don't worry about me, I can take care of myself."

The thought of Cooper getting hurt makes me want to be sick. "Be careful. Please."

He laughs and shakes his head. "I will, don't worry."

It hits me - it does now and again, that I'm sitting here, with Cooper. This is me. I'm being normal.

"If you would have told me I'd be sitting in a car with you having a conversation as though it's normal, I never would have believed it. I mean, God, I couldn't even talk to you a few weeks ago and look at me now."

"Well, of course, it's because I'm irresistible. Irresistibility trumps shyness."

I giggle. If only that were true. "Yes, Cooper you are irresistible."

It's been bothering me, since last week, that although we haven't had that much opportunity, there has been some, and he hasn't tried to kiss me again - not since his dad caught us. I'm dying to ask if it's because he doesn't want to, because his dad has said something, or if I'm just a terrible kisser.

I can't just blurt it out, he still seems interested in me because he texts me and wants to spend time with me. Does he see me as more of a friend now, after the kiss? I can't work him out.

I guess no time like the present. The answer can't be any worse than the answers I'm imagining.

"Cooper, you remember last week, with your dad?"

He glances at me, "Yeah..."

"Well, before your dad came in, we were kissing."

"Yeah, we were." His voice drops an octave.

I bite my lip. "We got a little carried away."

"I'll curse my dad forever for interrupting that."

I laugh, "So you liked it?"

"Are you crazy? Did it seem like I liked it?"

"Well, yeah, but since…"

"Since what?"

"Nothing." My face is burning and am glad it's dusk, hopefully, he won't be able to see, but who am I kidding? He's been around me enough by now to guess that I'll be the colour of a beetroot.

"Come on, you can't start this conversation and end it halfway through."

I take a deep breath. "I liked kissing you."

There I said it.

"And I liked kissing you."

He takes his hand and puts it on top of mine resting on my knee, doing my guitar thing. Total nervous tell, I need to stop doing that.

"So why haven't you done it again?" My voice sounds way too high pitched to be mine.

He is quiet for a moment and turns into the road where he pulls over, near the shop. He stops the car and takes it out of gear, turning to me. "I wasn't sure you wanted me to. After what happened with my dad, and you panicked, I thought you might regret it, so I wanted to give you time to get your head around it and I didn't want to come on too strong."

That makes sense, but I wish he'd have talked to me, I've been stressing all week and wondering why he hasn't tried to kiss me.

"That's nice of you."

"Too nice?"

I smile, "Maybe."

"Come here, then."

He leans forward and his lips brush against mine. His hand touches the side of my cheek in a barely-there touch, sending all my nerve endings on fire. Oh, I'm so into this guy. He smells so good, a mixture of wood and some male deodorant. I wish I knew what it was, I'd buy it and spray it all over my bedroom. I shouldn't be kissing him in his car on the corner of my street, but a whole Remembrance Day parade could march down here with a brass band and I wouldn't care. His lips are on mine, his hand is on my face, and that's all I care about.

It's only a brief kiss, but it's wonderful, and one that makes my heart happy because I know he wanted to kiss me but was giving me space, which makes him the sweetest guy ever. Oh yes, definitely falling for him. He breaks away and we stare at each other for a while, he gives a small smile.

"For the record, I always want to kiss you."

He shakes his head a little as though he can't believe he said that out loud. Inside I'm doing a dance that he did, and he called me his girlfriend tonight, even if it was to get rid of Ethan, it's a start.

Who would have thought that I had a chance with a guy that plays the drums and happens to be one of the hottest guys in school? Me, for cryin' out loud!

Chapter Eighteen

Cooper

Here it is, the school performance and I'm more terrified than I've ever been. Not for me. For her. I'm hoping with everything in me that she goes through with it. She is working backstage at the moment and is worryingly quiet. She's always quiet, but not with me. She is bottling everything inside and I hate it. All seems to be going according to plan, I'm expecting something to go wrong it always does, and then you deal with it, but up to now, all good.

People are arriving outside, and we are doing last checks: checking things are plugged in where they should be, that everyone knows who they're on after - which they should do because we've run through this like a hundred times, and checking the laptop set up for the music and lighting. We're good.

Christ, her nerves are contagious, I need to relax. But this is a big deal for her. She hasn't even told her parents she's performing. She wants it to be a surprise. They think they're coming to watch her run it and to listen to the song she helped write. They will be so proud of her.

I have no doubt when they see me, they will fire daggers at me. Metaphorical ones, although I'm sure they'd fire the real thing at me if they could. Heidi hasn't said anything, but they never apologised for treating me that way the night of the party, which I was a little disappointed at, but it's Heidi I'm bothered about - not them.

I need to talk to Charlie on the bus in the morning. I've done a little checking on this Ethan guy, and I heard he's on the rugby team with Charlie. I need to ask him what he knows about him. I have a feeling he's the guy that spiked her, but I need to be sure before I do anything about it. Makes my blood boil that some guy acts like it's okay to do that.

I see Heidi make her way backstage and follow her.

"Hey. You okay?"

Those gorgeous eyes are wide and full of fear. I want to hug her.

"Yeah. Actually, no. Big fat no. Am I crazy? Thinking I could do this? I'm punishing myself going through with this."

I put my hands on both her arms. "Hey, it's not punishment, it's guts. You have the guts to do this because you're sure it's what you want to do, and you don't want to keep living in fear for the rest of your life. You've got this. You can do it and you'll feel amazing when it's done. That you got out there in front of everyone and they heard you play. They will be mesmerised, same as I am when you play."

Her eyes soften, tears welling. "What if I mess up?" she whispers.

I lean in, so I'm close to her face, "You won't mess up. Trust me. I wouldn't encourage you to do this if I thought for one second you couldn't, but you're more capable than all of us."

She nods a little and takes a shaky deep breath. "Thanks."

I grin, "I could always find somewhere private for us to go and kiss you senseless if you want me to take your mind off it all."

She slaps my arm. "Are you crazy!"

I laugh. I was joking - well, unless she took me up on it, of course. In that case, I was totally serious.

Come on, Heidi, you can do this.

I'm worried she's going to pass out. It's here, our moment. And now we're here, in front of a silent audience that's waiting for us to start. I'm doubting that she's going to be able to do it. All the colour has drained out of her and her eyes won't go anywhere but the floor. I need to start the song, but she's not ready.

I say quietly, "Ready, guys?"

I get a nod from Ben and a smile from Annabel, but from Heidi? Nothing. This is not good.

"Heidi?"

I hear someone in the audience cough reminding me they're all watching, I need to do something quickly. I step out from behind my drums and go to stand in front of Heidi, turning to face her, to block her view of the audience. She looks at me when I get there. I see her defeated eyes, and my heart sinks.

"You can do this Heidi, you can."

She shakes her head. "My heart is beating so fast. A full-on panic attack is coming."

"Don't let it beat you."

The crowd must be wondering what is going on. Tough, they'll have to wait.

"I can't help it."

"Yes, you can." I grab her hand and put it flat on my chest. "Take a deep breath and feel my heartbeat. Close your eyes."

"People are watching."

"They can't see, I'm blocking their view. Don't worry about them. Close your eyes and concentrate on my heartbeat."

She closes her eyes slowly and takes a shaky breath in. My gut clenches when a tear rolls down her face. She feels defeated. Well, hell no, not on my watch. I place my hand over hers and breathe slowly.

"You got this, you are amazing and you can do this, you will rock this room."

She opens her eyes and exhales through her mouth. "Okay," she nods.

I see it come over her. The determination. She straightens her shoulders and her stance changes as she repositions the guitar.

I grin. "Well, okay, gorgeous."

I sit and start my countdown, ready to give the audience the show they've been waiting for.

I walk towards the bus stop in the morning, half on a high from last night, half worried about Heidi. What a performance! We were awesome. No one could believe how good we were together, especially as we literally only decided on it two days earlier. It worked. Boy did it work. The audience all stand at the end. And Heidi, well, she rocked it, last night took her to rock chick status for sure. She was brilliant. Once she began, all the nerves disappeared, and she went for it.

I was so proud of her, and still am. I didn't see her after the show as her parents came over and she left, I saw a few people congratulate her on the way out. I'm a little gutted she didn't come over, I guess she wanted to go straight to her parents. Still, an acknowledgement would have been nice. It's like she didn't want her parents to see me with her. She should be introducing us by now. Something I need to talk to her about, I thought all that was sorted.

I texted her last night to say congrats, but got no response, which is weird. I hope she's okay.

I see Charlie walking towards the bus stop on his phone. Now is my chance. Ed and Harper were still at Harper's when I set out, earlier than usual, in the hope I could speak to Charlie.

"Charlie, just the guy."

He smiles, "Oh, hey."

"I want to ask a favour of you."

He grins. This guy is always so happy. "Of course, my man, what's up?"

"Well, you're on the rugby team, right?"

"Yeah, someone told me it'd get me all the chicks but I'm still waiting."

I laugh, "Well, I was wondering what you knew about Ethan? He's on the team, right? He's in Heidi's year."

"Yeah, he's year eleven, the year above me, so I've not talked to him that much, but I can't say I'm a big fan of him."

"Why not?"

He shrugs, "Dunno, he's always talking about parties and drinking, trying to be the big guy."

"He drinks?"

Charlie nods, "Yeah, he says he can get it from his brother and drinks all the time. But not sure how much is true; he's probably trying to show the others his testicles are the biggest. He's one of those."

I nod, I know the type. "Could he have spiked Heidi?"

His eyes widen, "Shit, I'm not sure, he's a bit of a dick, but not sure he'd do that."

"Have you ever heard him say anything about Heidi?"

He shakes his head, "No, can't say I have."

"Don't suppose I could ask you to sound him out, could I?"

"How do you mean?"

"Well, Heidi's trying to find out who did it, it's important to her."

He nods, "I get that, I don't blame her. But what do you want me to do?"

"Not much, just sound him out about Heidi, mention her and see if he says anything then let me know. I don't want you to have to get involved but if he might be the guy, I can form a plan of action."

He nods, "Yeah sure, that was a lowlife thing to do what happened to her, if I can help you nail the guy that did it, I'm all for it."

I nod, "Thanks, bro."

I see the others approach and take a step back, happy that I've done something to help. It's a start.

Chapter Nineteen

Heidi

"Now you think on, no talking to that boy. Do you understand?"

I sigh and fight rolling my eyes, "Yeah, dad. I understand."

What a night last night was. I was on such a high when the song finished. Oh my god, I've never felt anything like it. But then I saw my parent's faces in the crowd, expecting them to be beaming with pride. Instead, they were livid. At first, I was confused, wondering what they had to get angry about, but then it twigged. Cooper's pep talk. We looked way closer than band members. Anger began to build in me. How can they think it's okay to treat him, and me, like this?

I should still be on that high, so happy. But all that has happened is I've gotten grief because my parents knew, as soon as Cooper came to me, they knew something was going on between us. Never mind that he helped talk me down from a panic attack, well, not just helped, he was the reason I didn't have one. They don't care about that. Dad doesn't even believe in bloody panic attacks anyway, so he doesn't think it's any big deal what Cooper did. Argh. Why won't they listen to me? And mum? She's taking his side.

I performed in front of a hall full of people.

Do they care? No, not one bit. Here's me thinking they'd be over the moon that I did that. Instead, all they care about is that there is a boy on the scene. They don't trust me, or my judgement, they think they can still speak for me, and what leg do I have to stand on? Dad says, his house, his rules. And his number one rule? No talking to Cooper. I've never felt hatred towards them before, but I'm so disappointed in them. You always think your parents are right, well not this time. They won't even listen to reason.

So now, I'm grounded. No phone either. I wonder if Cooper texted me? This is so unfair on him; I think I'm being treated badly, but what about him? He's done absolutely nothing wrong. And he'll be wondering what the hell is going on, I should have told him that Mum and Dad have no idea I'm seeing him, been honest with him, because he will be wondering why I didn't go over to him after the show. It's awful that I didn't. He would have been as excited as me that I completed that song. Knowing that he will have been looking for me afterwards guts me. I should have been celebrating with him instead of getting frog-marched out of there.

I need to talk to him. I should be buzzing about the show, instead, I have a big knot in my stomach and want to run the other way.

"Can I have my phone back? What if I need it?"

Mum shakes her head, "Your dad says no dear, you can borrow someone else's if you need to call us."

I sigh, they are taking this way too far. "I can't believe you're siding with him."

Her face has guilt written all over it, but dad steps in, "Of course she is because she agrees with me, and we are the grown-ups. Now get to school and I want you straight home too."

I grab my bag and walk out, not saying bye, barely staying calm. I haven't got a clue what to do, I need to see Cooper. They can't stop me from seeing him at school.

When Sara and I arrive, Cooper is waiting for me at the gates, leaning on the railings, looking gorgeous as always. My heart flips and hurts at the same time. I like him so much, in fact the bond I have with him is stronger than like, but why is he wasting time with me when my parents are reacting to him like they are? I should do him a big favour and walk away, but the thought of doing that makes me want to cry.

I walk over to him, "Hey."

He straightens, "Hey, I wanted to get you before you went in. Did you get my text?"

I shake my head and look to Sara, "I'll see you in form." She smiles at me sadly and carries on walking into school.

I look back at him, "There's something I need to tell you." My mouth goes dry, I don't want to admit this to him, it makes my parents sound like terrible people, which at the moment, I agree with, but I also have to admit I lied. So, this is not gonna go well for me. And after he was the sweetest guy in the world on stage last night too.

"What's up?" he sounds worried.

Here goes...

"Well, Mum and Dad were mad after they saw you with me on stage. I... I sort of never told them that you and I were, well whatever we're doing."

"Why not? You said they understood about the party night, they've been told it wasn't me."

"This is the part where I'm a terrible person. I lied about that. They wouldn't believe me." I take a swig of my water bottle; my mouth is so dry.

"What? Why?"

"Because I didn't want you to think bad of them, or that I was more trouble than I was worth."

He shakes his head. "I can't believe you lied to me. Ever since, you've been lying to me?"

"I'm sorry. But now they know something is going on and they don't approve. Obviously. They've taken my phone off me too."

His eyes flash with anger. "You are kidding me?"

I shake my head. "I never thought they'd be like this with me. They're treating me like a little kid. I'm sixteen, for god's sake."

"Yeah, well that's because they think I'm Lucifer, right? The big bad wolf coming to harm their daughter," He snaps.

"I'm sorry."

He shakes his head. "I can't believe you lied to me about this."

What do I say? I'm a terrible person. Besides him being mad at me, if by some miracle he wasn't, when would I actually see him if my parents won't let me?

"I feel terrible. We won't be able to hang out anymore after school, not for the foreseeable future. I'm totally grounded apart from to and from school because they presumed I've been seeing you and hid it. Which is true, so they're right."

"You know what, Heidi, with what I've just found out, that you've been lying to me all this time, I'm fine with not seeing you out of school. You're not the person I thought you were."

My legs turn to jelly. I can't bear him being mad at me. "I am, Cooper, I didn't want you to feel bad that they thought that of you."

"No, you wanted to carry on seeing me, so you out-weighed the risks and decided you'd keep it to yourself. Bad move. I hate liars."

My heart falls to my feet. Oh god, this is going way worse than I expected. "Hey, please don't be like that. I'm sorry. I should have told you."

"Yeah, you should have. I have to go."

"Will you meet me at dinner?"

He shakes his head. "No Heidi, I need to get my head around this, around the fact that you're a different person than I thought you were, and a bloody good liar, which is not a good thing. I'm going."

He turns around and I watch him leave as I stand there in the middle of the yard.

What have I done?

I've made a mess of everything.

As soon as I walk through the door when I get home, Mum is there. I was hoping she'd be at the library.

"Hey sweetheart, how was your day?" She looks nervous.

Is she serious?

"It was crap, thanks for asking."

She sighs. "What are we supposed to do? That boy brought you home in that state and you expect us to be happy that you're hanging around with him."

Well thanks to them, he doesn't want to hang with me anymore. Well, maybe because of me too, because I was an idiot and lied. "I don't want to talk about it. There's no point, I'd be wasting my breath because you won't listen and you don't trust me. After everything we've been through, I can't believe you're being like this with me. Our relationship was a lie, we've always been so close but now I understand it's because I've always gone along with everything you've wanted me to do. But this once, I know I'm right. And you don't like it. You've upset me more than Dad about this because Dad will always be Dad, he won't change, but you've always had my back."

"Please don't say that, love. Of course we're close." Her voice breaks.

"Yeah, because I've always been the dutiful daughter that did what she was told."

"No, don't be silly. What is so special about this boy, anyway?"

Anger rises inside me.

"You want to know what's special about him? He knows all about my anxiety and instead of running away he wanted to learn about it so that when I have an episode, he can help me. He listens to me, he says I'm special and talented. He's the kind of guy that when I freeze in front of a room full of people, he talks me down, calms me, because he understands how important it is to me to not let it beat me. He's perfect, mum!"

"Yeah, well, they all say what they want you to hear."

"He's not like that. But you wouldn't know, you haven't even given him a chance. You formed your opinion of him, and you won't change it. You saw what he did. You saw I was on the verge of having a panic attack and melt down in front of everyone and he stopped it, he calmed me down. How many guys his age, or any age, would do that?"

She looks guilty. She gets it, she gets what a big deal it was for him to do that.

"He's the reason I could perform up there at all. Yeah sure, I pushed myself to do it, but he's the one telling me how amazing I am and how I have to share it." I shake my head, "I'm going upstairs. I have no phone so don't worry I won't be speaking to him, not that he wants to speak to me after last night, anyway."

She doesn't say anything as I make my way upstairs.

It's going to be a long night.

I sit on my bed and look around. Hmmm. You know when you have an idea forming that you know is bad, but it keeps growing and growing until you do something about it? Well, I'm already in trouble, right? I could go to Connor's party tonight. Ethan will be there, I could talk to him, maybe sound him out to see if he was the one that spiked me. If I could get to the bottom of this, if nothing else it will make mum feel bad about how they acted towards Cooper and give me closure. I'm sick of looking around school, wondering who could have done that to me.

I sneak downstairs for my phone. Mum and dad are watching TV, they tried to get me to join them, but I didn't want to. I find it in the kitchen drawer, grab it and sneak back upstairs. They'd never believe their perfectly behaved daughter would do something like this, probably why they didn't hide the phone. Well, they pushed me too far.

I get back into my room and message Harper. "Hey. You going to Connor's party?"

Harper: Yeah, why? Don't tell me you're allowed to go?

I filled her in and she is gutted for me about Cooper, she understands why he's upset though, she asked me to come clean with him lots of times, and I should have. It all boils down to fear. I was scared that he'd give up on me. That I wouldn't be worth it. The trouble is, if all this happened again, I'd probably make the same mistake again because I still don't understand why he's showing an interest in me at all.

Me; No. Not exactly, but if I somehow get out, we can talk to Ethan?

Harper: Er yeah, but how do you plan to do that?

Hmmm, how can I do it? I could do the usual that I've seen on TV so many times. Lumps under the duvet, say I'm going to bed early like half nine and sneak out down the stairs and out through the garage. If I'm super quiet, they'll be watching TV in the living room, they won't have moved. It's risky as hell but I can get back in that way too. I'd be in and out before they even realise. Sod it, I'm doing it. I'll never sort this out if I don't do something, and I ain't staying in this bedroom for the rest of my life.

I'll go downstairs, act normal-ish, sit with them for a while, then tell them I'm watching a film in my room. If I go down for snacks right before I leave, they won't suspect a thing.

Me; Leave that with me. Can I meet you on Glover Street?

HarperSure, what time?

Me; Half nine? I get it's late, but that's the earliest I can manoeuvre it?

Harper; Yeah, that's fine. Is it okay if Ed comes?

Me; I take it you've told him our plan.

Harper; Yeah, sorry, I tell him everything and I wasn't giving away anything personal.

Me; Sure, as long as he's okay with what we're trying to do then it's fine.

HarperYeah, he might help.

MeDoes he hate me?

HarperNo.... but he's gonna have his brother's back. He'll be fine don't worry, Cooper will too, once he's calmed down. It was only a white lie after all.

Yeah, one that makes a difference, apparently.

Me; Right, will expect hostility from your boyfriend.

HarperDon't worry about him. See you in a while.

Right... operation 'sneak out of the house' needs to be put into action.

Chapter Twenty

Heidi

W e walk into the party and look around. It's rowdy and noisy, and I still don't know how Connor gets away with these parties. He has them every couple of weeks, his parents go out, they obviously don't care what he gets up to, and they're aware of the parties, but as long as they don't get backlash from them, they don't care. Great parenting.

Ed leans into Harper and says something and she nods, he walks off.

"Where's he going?"

"He's seen the basketball lot, so he's hanging with them for a while. Right. Where do we start?"

"Maybe look for someone that seems drunk? You know, happier than usual, and see if they got their beer from someone?"

She nods, "Good idea, come on, let's go through to the kitchen."

God, I hope mum and dad don't realise I'm missing. Sneaking out of the house was easy but something that makes me sick to my stomach. I've never gone against them before, I've always been the perfect daughter and followed the rules.

They shut the door to the living room, so the TV doesn't disturb me and to keep the heat in, and the key was in the garage door, which is now in my pocket, so I have my way back in. My heart was hammering in my chest as I was heading downstairs, praying one of them didn't creak. Which is crazy, because they'd have only thought I was getting a drink or something. But no creaking at all. If you go downstairs at a snail's pace on your tip toes, it seems to work!

We enter the kitchen and I see all the rugby guys at one end around the dining table. They're loud and boisterous as usual. Is that because they've been drinking? I mean, they're like that at school, so how am I supposed to tell?

She leans in, "Is Ethan with them?" She nods towards the rugby team.

I glance but don't want to make it obvious. "I'm not sure. I don't want to stare."

She sighs, "Well, no time like the present, let's talk to them."

My eyes go wide. "Now?"

"When were you thinking?"

"I don't know... never?"

"Ha ha, come on." She steps forward to go over and I grab her arm to stop her.

"Wait! Won't they find it weird us going over to them? We've never spoken to them properly before?"

She shakes her head, "I sit next to one of them in English and we get on, he's there, so I'll strike up a convo with him."

That sounds workable. I nod and we make our way over.

As we approach, we hear one of them saying, "She doesn't stand a chance when I ask her out, come on, who can resist this?"

What is it about rugby lads? They all think they're god's gift to women. They're not. I roll my eyes inwardly.

Harper nudges one of the boys, "Hey, how's it going?"

He smiles when he sees her, he has a friendly smile. "Harper, hey. You okay?"

"Yeah, a little bored. What are you up to?" she gives him one of her show-stopping smiles. It's a good job guys at school know she has a boyfriend, or he would totally think she was flirting.

He nods towards the guys, "Talking crap as usual." He seems nicer than the others.

He looks over at me. "Hey, Heidi."

I'm surprised he knows my name, "Oh hey...er...?"

"Gavin." He smiles.

"Hey, Gavin."

See, I'm totally a bad-ass when it comes to talking to boys now. You can't shut me up.

"You enjoying the party?" his eyes are shining. He's attractive, nice and tall.

I shrug, "Sure."

Charlie comes sauntering over, I've seen him talking to Harper and spoken to him a couple of times. He gets the bus with her in the morning. He is on the rugby team too but he's in a year below us.

Harper spots him. "Charlie! How are you doing?"

He shakes his head. "I'm trying to be irresistible, but all the girls keep resisting me. I don't get it. I'm charming right?"

She laughs. "Yes, Charlie, you are *very* charming."

I look at him. He has changed recently. He's lost weight, must be all the rugby, and he's taller. With his dark hair and green eyes, he's actually attractive, which I've never noticed before. He must sense me looking at him and he dips his head in greeting, "Heidi, looking gorgeous tonight, as always."

I blush and look down. "Thanks," I mutter.

Gavin turns to stand with Harper and I and Charlie, he leans into us, "Is Ed here?"

Harper nods, "Yeah, he's with his friends. We wanted to have a chat with you guys."

Gavin frowns, "Oh yeah? What about?"

"Well, I'm not sure if you were at George's party, but something happened with Heidi."

His eyes come to me, with what seems like sympathy. "Yeah, I heard what happened, I'm sorry someone did that. What a low life."

"Yeah thanks, it was horrible," I mumble.

He frowns and looks back at Harper. "What has this chat got to do with that?"

Harper opens her mouth to speak and Charlie interrupts. "Oh my god Harper, I totally forgot, I need to tell you something, did you see what Kins did on the bus? Have you heard what she's getting up to?"

We both frown at Charlie. Why is he changing the subject?

He grabs her arm. "I've got to tell you, come over here." He turns to Gavin. "We'll catch you later, man."

Gavin frowns and gives him a barely-there nod but says nothing and turns back to the guys.

We follow Charlie outside, where it's cool but not cold, and a few others are hanging out around. He takes us to a quiet corner.

He leans in. "I know what this is about and why you're asking; you're trying to find out who spiked you."

I frown, "Yeah, actually."

She shakes his head, "You can't just go up to any guy on the rugby team and ask about this. Gavin's a good guy, but rugby guys stick together. I shouldn't be talking to you about this, but Coop's already asked me to look into this for him and us bus guys have to stick together."

My mouth drops open, "Has he?"

"Yeah, the other day. He thinks it's Ethan."

I nod, "Yeah. I'm not so sure, but he's convinced."

Charlie carries on, "Well, at first I dismissed it. I thought there was no way that he would do that, even though he can be an arse sometimes, and he's always bloody bragging about different things, I didn't think he'd stoop so low. But..."

"But what?" Harper asks, leaning in.

"Well, when we'd finished training last night, I brought you up, Heidi, in casual conversation. Turns out, he has a bit of a thing for you."

I nod, "He's asked me out a couple of times, kind of."

"Yeah, well I'm downplaying it, when I say a bit of a thing, I mean he likes you, like a lot, once I mentioned you, he couldn't stop talking about you. About how he's going to get you to come out of your shell and get you over the shy thing. So, I mentioned the party where you got spiked and he said something like how you loosened up that night, and you could do with having a drink again."

"Yeah, so?"

Charlie shakes his head and speaks quietly, "Then he said, whoever spiked her drink did her a favour, she needs to loosen up."

I gasp and Harper says, "What an absolute arsehole!"

Charlie nods, "Yeah, I dunno, I got a bad feeling. The way he was talking about you, he likes you way more than is healthy. I was gonna talk to Cooper about it on Monday."

"Yeah, I wouldn't bother, we've kind of broken up, if we were ever together."

"So, you've had a row, so what?" Charlie shrugs.

"It's a little more than that."

"He cares about you Heidi, I could tell, he's into you big time so if you want to sort it out, I'm sure you will."

"I lied to him about something." Saying it out loud makes me sound so terrible.

He nods, "Well, do some sort of grand gesture, something to show how much you actually care. I'm sure you had your reasons for lying."

Yeah. Selfish reasons.

"Thanks, Charlie."

Harper speaks, "Thank you, o wise one, for your relationship advice, because you are such a guru."

He puts his hand on his heart. "Ouch, you know how to get me where it hurts."

She tilts her head and pats his arm. "Aw, I don't mean it!"

He gives her a big grin. "I knew it, you secretly love me, not Ed."

"Yeah, course I do." She rolls her eyes.

He gets serious. "Anyway, honestly? I think he did it."

Harper shakes her head, looking mad and turns to me. "You know what this means?"

I frown. "What?"

"It means that your gonna have to talk to him, pretend you're interested or whatever and get him to admit what he did."

"But that would be his word against mine."

"Ooh, I know," she says, her voice rising an octave, "you can put your phone on voice record in your pocket."

"I don't have it. Mum and Dad have taken it off me."

Harper shakes her head, "Jesus, they're strict. Here, borrow mine."

I take it off her. "But it's so noisy in there, no way our conversation would pick up on a recording."

Harper makes a face, but I'm not sure what it means.

I'm scared to ask... "Harper, what are you thinking?"

"You won't like it, but you'll have to get him to come out here." She scrunches her face in disgust.

"Oh god no. He'll think I'm coming on to him."

"It's the only way you'd be able to hear what he's saying. You'll have to make it seem like you're interested."

I take my glasses off and rub my eyes. "Oh Jesus, I'll never be able to do this, and what if he tries to kiss me or something?"

"Well, me and Ed will come out here, pretend we're kissing..."

Charlie snorts, "Pretend? That's all you do!"

"Shut up!" She turns to me, "We will be nearby, so you'll be safe, but not so near as he suspects its planned.

I bite my lip. If I do this, it will go a long way to helping my situation. It will mean that my parents have to believe me when I tell them Cooper is innocent and it will hopefully show Cooper that I'm serious about my feelings for him. If nothing else, if he never speaks to me again, it's important to me to clear his name with my parents. It doesn't change the fact that I lied to him, but it makes it a little less trouble to be with me. And no lies are needed to anyone anymore. I have to do this. Plus, I need closure. I don't like having the power taken away from me like that, and not having a clue who did it does mess with my head, so it would be nice to find out for myself too.

"Right, I'll do it. I need to do it. Let's get this sorted." I turn to Charlie, "He's here, right?"

He nods, "Yeah, somewhere."

I turn to Harper, "Okay, you go tell Ed the plan and I'll find Ethan and bring him to this spot, so come and stand nearby."

Charlie rubs his hands together, "Oh, this is so exciting!"

"And you, keep your lips sealed, yeah?" I say to Charlie.

Harper looks at me her mouth open, "Who are you and what have you done with Heidi?"

I realise I got carried away, "Oh sorry Charlie, what I meant to say was thank you for all your help I owe you one."

He shakes his head, "No problem, I'd ask you on a date, but I guess you're pretty hung up on the moody twin, right?"

I smile, "Yeah, 'fraid so."

He shakes his head as he walks off muttering, "Story of my life."

We make our way inside and I Ethan in the living room talking to someone I've never seen before, and a girl is standing with them. My hands shake as I lift out Harper's phone and put it on record and put the lock screen on and slide it into my jacket pocket.

Okay, it's now or never.

Chapter Twenty-One

Heidi

My heart is beating so fast as I make my way over to him. Come on Heidi, sort yourself out, this is just a conversation with a guy that you don't even like, who cares if you mess it up?

I take a deep breath and straighten my shoulders, walking over to him as confidently as I can.

When I reach them, the three of them look at me. Ethan raises his eyebrows when he sees it's me.

"Hey, Ethan," I croak.

"Heidi, hi, I didn't think you were here tonight."

I nod, "Yeah Harper, Ed and I have just arrived. I was hoping to find you."

He looks at the other two who are watching our conversation, then back at me, "Were you?"

I nod and swallow, why is my mouth so dry? "Yeah, I wanted to talk to you. Have you got a minute?"

He nods, a little too eagerly, "Sure, you want to go to the kitchen?"

He turns to the other guys and says, "Catch you later."

When we arrive in the kitchen, luckily fate is helping me as it is so crowded in there, no way we could have a talk, so I lean into him, "Want to go outside?"

He looks like it's his birthday, as usually when you go outside it's for more than talk. "Yeah, let's do that."

He steps back and holds his arm out as if a gentleman letting a lady go first. I'm pretty sure he's no gentleman though. I walk outside and stand where I was talking with Harper and Charlie minutes ago. Hopefully, Harper has had enough time to find Edward and is on her way, I can't see her anywhere at the moment. Come on, Harper. I'd feel much better if she was nearby.

I turn to him and smile. I don't want to speak to him but I'm going to have to put all my shyness and nerves to one side if I want to do this, and it's important to me and to whatever Cooper and I have, I have to do it.

"I wanted to have a chat with you on your own."

He nods, "Cool, that's great. Are you having fun? I've been wanting to get you alone at a party for a long time."

I giggle. It sounds forced, probably because it is. I am so bad at flirting, especially when it's with a guy I don't like.

"To be honest, I've been avoiding parties for a couple of weeks, everyone was talking about me because of... well because of Henry's party."

He nods, "Yeah, you shouldn't care what people think. It's good to let loose once in a while."

I get an idea and decide to go with it. "Yeah, actually after that party I decided that myself."

"Yeah?"

I lean in and whisper, "I'm a little drunk right now."

He raises his eyebrows. "So that's why you're talking to me?"

I nod. "Gives you courage to talk to people, doesn't it? Do you drink?"

He nods, "Hell yeah, all the time. I like this, Heidi."

I tilt my head. I've seen Harper do it, it usually works. "Yeah? You do?"

"Yeah, I knew you just needed to loosen up."

My heart hammers harder. He steps in so that he's closer to me. "That night at the party, I was watching you, you looked tense, stressed out. I thought you might need a de-stress, so I was doing you a favour."

I get goosebumps - he's pretty much admitted it, but I need him to say the words.

"How do you mean?"

"Well, it was me that put some vodka in your drink. I knew once you loosened up, you'd appreciate it."

Bingo. What an absolute low life.

I look around and don't see Harper. Where are you?

He carries on, "So now you've decided you like how it feels. Maybe you should try other things too?"

He steps even closer, he was already closer than I liked, his face is inches away from mine. He's going to kiss me. Crap!

I take a deep breath. "Truth is, Ethan, I'm furious that you did that to me at the party. Do you have any idea how it feels to act a certain way and not know what's happened to you?"

"Actually, yeah, I like to do that all the time."

Yeah, I bet he does.

"Look, don't be mad, I just wanted you to relax." His hand goes to my hip and he tries to pull me into him. I hold my hand up and push on his chest. "No way, never," I hiss. Get me away from this guy.

A rage builds in my gut that I didn't think I had. How *dare* he do this to me?

He resists the push. "Hey, let's talk about this."

I shake my head as I hear a familiar voice,

"Get your hands off her!"

In a blur, Ethan is gone. What is happening? Is that Ed?

I look at the guy rolling around on the floor with Ethan. Is that? Is that Cooper? Oh my god. Cooper is here? And fighting with Ethan? Jesus, can this night get any worse?

I try to grab Cooper's shoulder to get him to let Ethan go but he shakes it off. I hear someone in the distance yell 'fight', and they draw a crowd. I breathe a sigh of relief when I see Edward and Harper running toward us.

"Ed, please help Cooper," I plead.

"I don't need help," he says through gritted teeth.

I see him rear his fist back and punch, Ethan bends double groaning. Oh god, he's hit him.

Ed grabs Cooper by the arms in a lock and pulls him back. "Stop, Coop, or all the rugby team will get involved."

"I don't care, let them!" he shouts

Cooper has lost it and the last thing I want him doing is getting hurt because of me.

I step in front of Cooper and his eyes drop to mine. I see nothing but distaste in them. "You were going to kiss him?" he hisses.

I gasp. He thinks I would do that? Does he think so little of me?

He shakes his head and shrugs Edward off, "Doesn't matter, I don't care." And then he walks off. Harper and Edward stare at me and the rugby guys come running over.

"What happened?" Gerard asks.

I point to Ethan. "He admitted to spiking my drink at the party."

He looks at Ethan. "Is this true?"

"No, it's not true, and she can't prove it. It's her word against mine."

Please let Harper's phone have recorded all this.

Edward steps forward and leans into him. I didn't know Edward could be intimidating, I was wrong. "You put alcohol in a girl's drink without her consent." He didn't make it sound like a question. It was a statement.

"Dude, back off him," one of the rugby guys says.

"No, leave them to it." Charlie appears. "It was uncool what he did."

The rugby guys are surprisingly quiet. At least they don't seem to agree with what he did.

Ed turns around and faces me. "Did you get it?"

I nod and hand him the phone, stopping the record button as I do. Edward takes the phone off me and holds it up. "Every single word as proof, all here recorded for all the world to hear."

He looks at Ethan. "So, I guess it's not your word against hers after all."

There are mumblings through the crowd and Ethan now looks terrified. He turns to me. "It was nothing serious, a bit of fun to loosen you up."

Gavin speaks, "I can't believe you did that."

Charlie shakes his head, "Man, you have any idea how bad that is?" He looks at me. "You alright?"

I nod. I'm trembling and I want to go home, but then I tremble more at the thought of trying to sneak back into the house.

Harper speaks, "We'll walk you home hun."

I nod and we leave, leaving all the mess for everyone else to sort out.

Once we get on the street Harper turns to me and embraces me in a hug. "That was intense. Are you sure you're okay?"

I hug her back for a moment. Glad it's over, then release her. "Yeah, at least I know who did it now and why. I guess nothing serious happened, but it will make me more aware of what I'm doing in groups of people. Lesson well and truly learned."

"I'm sorry we were late getting to you and that slime-ball tried it on with you. I couldn't find Ed anywhere, we kept missing each other, he was looking for me and I couldn't phone him."

I shake my head, "No harm done. Cooper was there."

"Yeah, what was that about him showing?"

I shrug, "I don't have a clue, he's never been to one of those parties before."

"He was there for you," Ed says quietly.

"He hates me," I mumble.

He snorts. "Obviously not."

I turn and look at him, "Do you hate me?"

He sighs and shakes his head, "Course I don't. You're one of the nicest people I know, Heidi. It just took me by surprise that you lied to him, I didn't think you had it in you."

"I've liked your brother for ages... years, even. Ironically, I didn't want to mess things up by telling him about my parents."

He nods. "I get it. Give him time."

People keep saying that. I hope it's true.

"Will you be okay? Are you going to talk to your parents now or in the morning?" Harper asks.

"I won't be able to sleep so I may as well do it now."

"Fair enough, at least they'll learn the truth and change their opinion of Coop."

"Yeah, I guess, but it won't help their opinion of me. This is scary - I thought confronting Ethan was bad. But telling my parents I snuck out, oh my god, they're gonna hit the roof."

"Yeah, but at least you've cleared Coop's name, that'll mean something," Ed says. I bet he hates my parents. I can't say I blame him. Everybody believes they are in the right here, including my parents. I'll never forget that they didn't trust me.

I say goodbyes to them both on the corner of my street and make my way back in through the garage. I go into the living room.

"Mum, Dad, I need to talk to you."

Chapter
Twenty-Two

♥

Cooper

I stay at home all weekend and only come out of my room when I have to. I can't believe I got in a fight over her. Will I ever learn? She lied to me, and looked like she wanted to kiss Ethan. I mean, sure, she was saying no, but why did she go in the garden with him in the first place? It doesn't make sense. I've been wracking my brains all weekend. I nearly phoned her, but why didn't she phone me? She could have at least called or texted to see how I was after defending her honour or whatever.

Ed and Harper have been unusually quiet about it all. I haven't seen them much but when they have, they haven't mentioned Friday. Weird.

Maybe school today will shed some light on things. Something is going on.

When I walk into the kitchen, it's just Ed.

"Hey," I say, walking past him to grab a cereal bar.

"Hey, you gonna talk to Heidi today?"

I grab the bar I want and rip it open, taking a bit and lean on the counter. "What for?"

"Don't you want to know what was happening on Friday night?"

I shake my head, "Why would I?"

"Maybe because you started a fight for her, maybe you care."

"I shouldn't have started anything. I should have left her to it."

"Come on, dude, that Ethan is a lowlife, he was trying to kiss her, you did the right thing."

"Yeah, well, that doesn't seem to get me anywhere these days, does it?"

"Talk to her, there's stuff going on, but it's not for me to tell you."

I look at him. "What stuff?"

He shakes his head, "Just talk to her."

"At the risk of sounding like a girl, she didn't even try to call me this weekend to thank me for doing what I did, so maybe she didn't want to be interrupted like it seemed."

"Yeah, she did, Harper and I were supposed to be there but..."

What the heck? "Why were you and Harper supposed to be there?"

"Just talk to her, and by the way, she probably couldn't call you because her mum and dad have confiscated her phone."

Jesus, they are a piece of work. My mood lifts a little when I realise she couldn't phone me, but that doesn't change the fact that she lied to me. A lie that could have gotten me in serious trouble. If her parents had caught me with her, they would have presumed I was in on it and they hate me as it is. So no, I can't get over that. She always seemed so innocent, so naïve, so to find out that she has this conniving side to her, I don't like it. Not one little bit.

I sigh, "Fine, I'll talk to her today. Not that it'll change anything."

"Just try not to be so stubborn when you do."

It's halfway through the day before I see her. She looks gorgeous, she always does. I feel it in my gut. Why am I so drawn to her?

Because we have tons in common, she is super talent-ed, but most of all? She gets me because she's the same. Oh, and she's gorgeous and every time I see her and she smiles at me I want to kiss her. I have it bad. I need to know what's going on. I see her in the queue for lunch, she'll sit with our crowd. I look around, there is a grassy area where people who don't want to sit on the benches are sitting, there is lots of space, so we could sit there in private.

I walk over and make her jump when I say her name.

"Cooper, hi!" She stares at me but doesn't say anything.

"When you get your lunch, you fancy coming sitting on the grass with me? We should talk."

She nods. "Sure, do you want anything?"

"No, thanks, I grabbed a sandwich from sixth from the common room." I hold it up with my drink to show her. "I'll pick a spot, yeah?"

She nods, and I walk over to the grass and sit. I have my jacket which I lay next to me for her to sit on so she doesn't get her uniform dirty, the grass is dry, but still...

When she walks over, I pat my coat. Her eyes go to it and back to mine and she sits gingerly on it.

"What did ya get?"

"Thursday, chicken burger of course."

I smirk, the chicken burger at our school is world-famous, Thursdays are a busy day at the school canteen.

"They are good."

"Want a bite?" She holds it out to me with the foil pinned back.

It seems like an intimate gesture, her offering it to me, "sure." I lean forward to take a bite, they are the best.

We chew for a while in silence when she speaks. "Thank you, for helping me on Friday night when Ethan... well, when he was..." she can't find the words, so I help her out.

"When he was trying to grope and kiss you?"

212

She winces, "Yeah, don't remind me."

"But you wanted to be out there with him?"

"Only because I had to," she replies.

"Why did you have to?" Did he make her go outside? I'll kill him.

"Don't you know? I thought Ed would have filled you in?"

"Filled me in with what? What's going on?"

"I got him to admit, it was him, the party, spiking my drink. He admitted it all."

I shake my head, "You'd better start from the beginning, Heid, how did all this come about?"

She fills me in, the plan she and Harper had, her sneaking out, the phone recording - all of it.

"So, you didn't want to go outside with him, it was all part of the plan?"

"Urgh. No way. You didn't think I actually was interested in him, did you?"

"I didn't know what to think, and when you didn't even contact me this weekend..."

"Things haven't been good at home this weekend. In fact, things haven't been good for a while, but I had to tell them I sneaked to the party. They're not in a very forgiving mood."

"They didn't leave you much choice, did they?"

"They don't get it, they don't get how much you..."

She doesn't finish.

"How much I what?"

She shakes her head, "Doesn't matter now. So yeah, my parents kept my phone, and my freedom. I'm allowed to go to school and that's it. Partly because I snuck out and partly because they're terrified something like that will happen again but worse. That someone like you wasn't around to help."

"What's gonna happen with the recording?"

"Mum and Dad want to have a meeting with the head today, they're gonna play it for him. It happened out of school and Dad is talking about going to the police, which I'm not too sure is going to do me any favours."

Sadness washes over me that now all this is sorted, if she'd told me the truth, we might actually have something to work on. But between her lying to me and her parents not letting her out of their sight, there doesn't seem much hope.

"Why didn't you just tell me the truth?" I plead.

She looks down at her lap. "I'm sorry."

"I get that, but why did you do it?" I probe.

She looks at me, those honey eyes looking terrified. She opens her mouth to speak when we hear, "Heidi!" I turn around and the head is standing there with her parents.

"Oh, well, isn't this just perfect timing?" I mutter.

They're scowling at her as though she's the one that's done something wrong.

"Oh no, this is all I need. I better go." I watch her stand and walk over to them. The head says something, and they all walk off together. Harper watches it all and comes over and sits beside me.

"What's that about?"

"They want to see the head about the spiking."

She nods, "She fill you in on why she was with Ethan?"

I nod "Yeah." I flop onto my back and let the sun warm my face. "It's all a big mess."

"Yeah, it is, and she's one of the worst people it could happen to because her parents aren't the best at letting go of their little daughter."

I huff, "No, I get that impression of them."

"You like her?"

"I did, no, I do, but I'm not sure if I can get over the lying thing, and her parents won't let her out of their sight anyway."

"No, I need to do something about that."

"What can you do?"

She bites her lip. "I'm not sure, but I have to come up with something. If I don't, she's gonna end up either having a breakdown or rebelling altogether. Someone has to make them realise they're being crazy. They're like that because of her anxiety. Her mum has always been extra vigilant to keep away her triggers, but at this point now it's habit for her mum – she doesn't know how to be any different."

"I get it, but she's gonna go crazy and her relationship with her parents is gonna totally break down," I sigh. Like I say, a big mess.

"Her anxiety has been so good lately, I haven't seen her have a panic attack for ages and she seems more confident in her own skin."

"Yeah, she's more at peace with herself, doesn't look like there's a war going on behind those eyes of hers. Even though she has this shitstorm going on."

"It's you to thank for that."

My stomach clenches. "I don't know about that."

She nods, "It is, you've got her to believe in herself."

"I can't believe she didn't anyway, she's amazing, everything about her. Why is it so hard for her to believe?"

"Yeah, doesn't matter how many times I told her that, it didn't make any difference, but she seems to believe you. You're different too...since you started this thing with Heidi."

I squint at her through the sunshine. "Am I? How?"

"Dunno, you talk more. I feel closer to you and not cos of Ed, you're actually having a full conversation with me."

I guess she's right, maybe it's not just me bringing out the best in Heidi, maybe she brings out the best in me.

Harper gasps. "I've got it!"

"What?"

"I need to go to the toilet to text someone."

She stands quickly and dashes off. Another hair-brained plan of Harpers is being put into effect.

Chapter Twenty-Three

Heidi

I watch my sister walk up the path to our house. What is she doing here? She's not even due home. Always the golden girl, can't do no wrong, but I love the bones of her. She can't help being the favourite. She's my favourite too. Like the perfect version of what I should be, but I couldn't be more different.

Mum and Dad got stuck with me while she goes away to Uni. I run to the door and swing it open, yelping.

"What are you doing here?" I throw my arms around her and she hugs me back tightly. I didn't know how much I needed her right now. I've never been so fed up in all my life and that's saying something, as anyone with anxiety will tell you. We have a tendency to see the worst-case scenario in every situation, which doesn't actually make for a happy life!

"Came to see my little sis, of course!"

"You have no idea how good it is to see you." I hug her so tightly I'm going to cut off her circulation. It's like she knew I needed her. No perfect boyfriend, no social life, no actual lift right now - yup I needed her!

I release her and she watched me from arm's length. "Actually, I do. Are Mum and Dad home?"

I shake my head, "No, they've gone out for tea, they wanted me to go but I didn't want to." It's Thursday after the Ethan thing last Saturday and so much has been going on, the last thing I want to do is sit across the table from my parents and play happy families.

"Right, let's make a brew then sit. You can tell big sis all your problems."

I nod and go to walk into the kitchen but stop when I realise something, "So how did you find out that I've got all the problems in the universe right now?"

"Well, you have one good thing. Your friend Harper. She called me, filled me in and said that you need my help. So here I am, ready to get started."

Harper. I could cry. Warmth rushes through my body. She is such a good friend. She is trying to fix things for me as she tries to do for everyone - not sure this can be fixed but she cared enough to try and that means a lot.

After I've finished telling my story to Molly, she sits back and stares at me. "Jesus, Heidi, this sounds like a storyline from Hollyoaks or something. How has all this happened in the space of a few weeks?"

I shake my head, "Tell me about it."

She frowns at me and tilts her head to the side, "I'll tell you what though?"

"What?"

"Something has changed about you."

"How do you mean, changed?"

"You have all this going on, and probably the worst you've ever had it but look at you. Your nervous twitches, the things you do when you're stressed out, they're gone. You look, well, relaxed."

"Believe me, I'm anything but relaxed, but... I get what you're saying, I'm a lot better, with my anxiety, I've started to look at things differently, I have by no means beaten my anxiety, It's always there, you know?"

She nods. "I know, honey."

"It'll never go away but now... it's like I've realised that is exactly what it is, I recognise when it's my anxiety talking to me when it starts to build. Whereas before I thought it was a situation getting out of control, now it's like 'okay, crap-head, go away, I know what you're trying to do'. And most of the time? It goes away," I sigh, "I'm not explaining it very well, but yeah, it's like I've compartmentalised it for what it is, I can realise that it's not controlling me anymore, I'm controlling it, mostly."

"I'm so proud of you Heidi, this is massive, you get that right?"

I nod. I really do, it's life-changing for me. "I'm kinda proud of myself, I mean, I had help, but it's me that has ultimately got a handle on it. Like I said, it's never going away, but I've got a handle on it."

"You should be bloody proud of yourself." She shakes her head, frowning, "I don't get what is going on in mum and dad's heads. They should be over the moon for you. You're finally living the life a sixteen-year-old girl should live, instead of hiding away at home. You have this guy after you, who actually gets you," she leans into me, "who is absolutely gorgeous, by the way," I chuckle and she carries on. "You've played guitar on stage, I still couldn't believe It when I saw the video you sent me, and you got to the bottom of this spiking thing all on your own and yet mum and dad are being worse than ever. Well, not when I've finished with them."

My eyes go wide. She's always just gone with the flow, Her and our parents have never had a cross word, so the fact that she's going to stand up to them, for me, well it means the world.

"Thank you, I hope you get through to them, but I'm pretty sure it will be a wasted journey for you."

"Oh, I will get through to them, you'll see, and one; it will never be a wasted journey when I get to see you and two; it was worth coming home to see you like this. You're amazing, my rock chick sister is rocking the world."

I laugh. "I wouldn't go that far."

"So, once I get through to mum and dad, how are you gonna get back in Cooper's good books?"

This is something I've been trying to solve all week. He speaks to me when he sees me at school, but things have been weird for me at school this week. Ethan's parents got called in and all the school found out it was him. Everybody at school thinks he's out of order. Doesn't matter how tight-knit the rugby crew are, when one of them does something like this, they're out. So yeah, he's the school pariah at the moment. He isn't allowed to talk to me, but he hasn't gotten suspended or anything because we weren't at school when it happened. He has been moved, so he isn't in any classes with me, for my mental wellbeing, apparently. I'm worried he's going to confront me, but for now, he's being kept away, but that can't go on forever. I have a lot of people that have my back anyway and he would be an idiot to come near me. He has to stay in at break times for now and have lunch in solitude. His parents are horrified, and he's grounded at home. They've contacted mum and dad. So yeah, it's been a tense week at school.

But how do I get back into his good books? I'm unsure what to do, basically, he doesn't trust me anymore so there's not much I can do about that.

I realise Mol is waiting for an answer. "I haven't got a clue. Any ideas?"

"What is he into?"

I laugh. "Well, that's easy, music."

"Well, you could write him a song or something?"

I scrunch my nose. "No, too much pressure. He loves The Hideaway, maybe I could surprise him there with something, like a McDonald's and a drink, and he'd stay and talk to me."

"Heidi, that is the lamest thing I've ever heard, You are not gonna win him over with a MacDonalds!"

I raise my eyebrows at her, "You'd be won over."

She laughs and looks like she's thinking.

I get the most amazing idea. "Wait! I have an idea!"

"What?"

I shake my head, "No, I'm not gonna plan anything, I'll see how your talk with Mum and Dad goes."

She nods, "Fair enough, when are they due back?"

I look at the time, "Dunno, they might be a couple of hours yet."

"Time for a girlie movie and Haribo."

Sounds like a plan to me.

I hear dad's car pull into the drive and my relaxed state ends at once, I look at Molly. "Well, here we go!" she says, slapping her thigh.

We decide it's best if I go upstairs and she'll call me if I need to join in the conversation. I go up and sit and wait. I want to form my plan, but I can't do anything about it at the moment. I need an apology song for it though, I scroll through my favourite artists to see if any of their songs fit.

"Heidi, can you come here?" My sister shouts.

Oh god, here we go.

I walk into the living room and three pairs of heads swing in my direction. I have no way of telling from their faces which way the talk has gone.

"Sit down, Heidi, we want to talk to you."

I glance at my sister, who is smiling at me. That's a good sign, surely.

"Molly has been talking to us and she has made us realise something. We have been treating you differently than we treat her. Maybe we needed this spelling out to us before now, but she has told us some home truths. She said that you think we favour her over you. How could you think that?"

"Well, come on, she's the perfect daughter, right? I'm the one that has panic attacks and has to see a therapist."

Mum gasps, "That's terrible that you think that. Have we made you feel that way?"

"You haven't, Mum, not about the therapy, at least."

Dad speaks, "But I have?"

I shrug but don't speak, sometimes a shrug can work better than words.

Mum and Dad look at each other and Dad runs his hands over his head. "Heidi, I'm so sorry that you feel that way."

I sigh. "You can't help it."

"I'll do something about it, I promise."

I nod.

"So... this boy."

"You mean Cooper?"

Mum nods. "You like him?"

I shrug and glance at Molly not sure how much she's told them. "I don't like the way you treated him."

"Oh honey, you'll see when you have kids of your own. We just want you safe."

"I'm sixteen, mum, you let Molly go out when she was sixteen."

"Well yeah, but she wasn't interested in boys, Molly, was and is all about the study, so this is the first time we've had to deal with it."

Gee, thanks Mol, why couldn't you have been more interested in boys?

"Okay, but do you not get that you can trust me?"

Dad speaks. "I know what goes on in a teenage boy's mind, I used to be one."

I try to keep calm. "I'm sure you do, and I'm not saying he's not thinking those things, but he isn't asking me to do any of them. We like the same things, we have a lot in common and I like him. These past few weeks when all this has been going on, he helped me. If you saw how I was in the first music meeting, when I fainted, remember?"

Mum nods.

"Well, he was the one that took me to the nurse's office and he totally gets it, well he didn't, but he learned about it so he got it. He cares about me. Or he did."

"Did?"

"He found out I lied to him about you guys, he thought you were fine with us seeing each other and doesn't like that I lied."

"So, all the time we've been worried about this boy taking you off the rails and it was the other way around?" dad asks.

Molly laughs.

I snort, "Something like that."

"Well, for what it's worth, if you work it out with him, we will give our permission for you to see each other." She sighs and looks at Dad, "Either way, we owe him an apology, don't you agree? He was the one that helped her when that happened to her and we've treated him terribly."

"Yeah, we will," my dad says wearily.

"Stop treating me with kid gloves. I'm leaving school this year, I mean, the sixth form yeah, but just because I have anxiety, doesn't mean you can't let me act my age. I've got a handle on that at the moment, I'm not saying I always will, not by any means, but for now, I'm good, so let me be a sixteen-year-old girl."

"Well said, sis. What do you two say?"

They both nod and mumble their agreement. Have I actually gotten somewhere with them? They're gonna let me see Cooper? How ironic that now he doesn't want to see me because I lied to him about them agreeing to see me. Wow, that's complicated. Still, I'm glad my sister got through to them. I guess time will tell if it sticks.

Molly turns to me. "Right, come on, upstairs, we have some planning to do."

Chapter Twenty-Four

♥

Heidi

"So, this girl, Jen, she will help you out?" Molly asks.

I nod, "I'm sure she will, I clicked with her and she is the type that will help, for sure. I have her number, she gave it to me last time I was there."

I pick up my phone and message her.

Me; Hey, it's Heidi, I have a problem with Cooper and I'm wondering if you'd be able to help me with it. Can I call you?

As soon as I send it, my phone rings. It's Jen.

I explain to her what is going on, and just as I knew she would be, she's totally on board with the idea of playing something for him. She said that Saturday afternoon I should get my friends to The Hideaway and she will get Jay to get Cooper to go.

Once I end the call from her and fill Molly in, the nerves kick in big time.

Oh my god I'll have to sing in front of my friends. I mean, technically, they don't have to be there, but when they find out what's going on, I'm not going to be able to keep them away. Plus, they'll be my moral support, keeping me going until I have to do this. I have to do this. What if he laughs at me though and walks out? No, he would never laugh, but he might walk out. I have to keep my fingers crossed that he likes me enough to look past the lying thing and that he can trust me. I have to find the perfect song.

My mission, if I choose to accept it (and I do) is to find the perfect song, perform brilliantly and end up winning over the guy I've been crushing on for years. The mission begins now...

Saturday comes around way too quickly. Harper has come to mine at the crack of dawn along with Sara. They're worried I'm a flight risk. My sister can't make it but has made Harper promise to video it all. It will be recorded for the rest of my life! Even though she has promised not to share it with anyone, it's still digitally recorded.

I found it though. The perfect song. I trawled through hundreds of songs to find the perfect one. I wanted it to be music that we both would listen to, not a chart pop song. Liam Gallagher pulled it out of the bag for me. The track is called For What It's Worth and it's all about how sorry he is, he could have written the song for me honestly. Oasis was the band back in the day, but Liam has done some amazing solo stuff. But yeah, that song hits it right on the head, so I've done nothing but practice and learn it since I discovered it. I've got it nailed as long as I don't forget the words. Jay is playing guitar for us, but that means I have nothing to do with my hands when I'm singing, so I guess I'll be holding on to the mic for dear life.

Then there was the outfit. It also had to say I'm sorry. How can an outfit say that? Well after going around a hundred clothes shops, I've decided they can't say any-thing, they're just clothes. But I wanted to look good, so picked out some black leather-look leggings and a halter neck top that goes with my bobbed hair - don't ask me how, it just does. It's a cute look that goes well together, sort of a girlie contrast with some rock chick thrown in. My hair and make-up will be the same as always. I'm just me at the end of the day.

When I walk into The Hideaway, Derek strolls over to me. "Heidi! Good to see you."

He looks behind me, where Harper, Ed and Sara are behind me. "You brought friends."

I nod, "I did, I hope it's okay. They wanted to come and support me."

Jen had told Derek about my plan, he thought it was a great idea, he said we could do whatever we need to. He seems to have never-ending patience. I have only seen him here a couple of times, he only pops in every so often. Trust him to be here now when I have to sing!

"Absolutely fine, I like to have it busy in here and you never know, they might want to come back sometime." He looks past me at them, "Guys, make yourself at home."

They all smile at him and say thanks and I lead them over to a table. Once they're settled and I've told them where to get drinks, I go to find Jen. She texted me to say she was already here, I just can't see her. I'm heading towards the stage when I see her coming out of the ladies, she bounces over to me. "I'm so freaking excited about this, it's proper dramatic." She clutches her chest, "True love will prevail," she says, looking off into the distance.

I bloody hope so!

I smile at her; her enthusiasm is contagious. "Did you speak to him, did he say he's coming?"

She nods and looks at her phone, "Yeah, I told him we had a singer for his band, and obviously he doesn't think you'll be doing it anymore, so he's all over it, wanted to come straight away, I had to tell him that she can only get here later."

How can I be jealous of this 'singer girl', when it's me. I'm obviously losing it.

"Oh brilliant, he'll have his hopes up and then see me standing there."

"What are you talking about, you're the new singer of his band, right?"

I stare at her. Is she serious?

"Um, no."

"Yeah, well see."

"You haven't even heard me sing." She wasn't here at the time I did it.

She shrugs, "True, you could be crap, but somehow I doubt it."

I'm glad she has faith in me, but the pressure is immense about now.

I set up on stage and hang with the guys a little. Then the rest of the band get here, Jay and Ben, who chat with me for a while, I've met them a few times, and they have grins on their faces the whole time. They're finding all this so amusing, some silly little spat between me and Cooper... cute even. They couldn't be more wrong; this is a big deal for me. Still, they're going along with it, that's the main thing. I messaged them what I was going to sing, but we have time to rehearse before he comes in, thank God. How nerve-wracking would it be to do it for the first time in front of him?

And of course, right on cue, in walks Cooper. My heart stops. What is he doing here?

I jump down from the stage and run into the ladies, which is a door at the side of the stage and ring Jen.

She answers. "Heidi?"

"I'm in the ladies, get in here as quick as you can. Cooper is here."

"Oh shit." She says and ends the call.

The door swings open and she crashes in. "What the hell is he doing here so early?"

Like I'm going to know the answer to that one.

I shake my head, gobsmacked.

She drums her fingers against her lips, "Maybe I made his new singer sound a little too good, got him all worked up and he needs to work on his drumming or something, let off some steam," she cringes.

Okay, now getting even more jealous.

She carries on. "I'm sorry I had to make up a sure way to get him here and I knew if I hold him we had a singer for the band, he'd be champing at the bit to get here. I never thought that he might come early though."

"What do I do now?"

She looks at me blankly, "What do you mean?"

"Well, I can't sing now, can I? The band and I haven't even practised. You're supposed to be standing in for Coop on the drums while I sing, but you said yourself, you're a novice and you haven't even heard the track live, never mind practised."

She shrugs, "Ah, don't worry about that, I'll wing it, I've listened to it loads since you sent me the link, I've got it. I don't like to follow music sheets or anything anyway."

"But the drums control the whole song."

She chuckles, "Heidi, relax, I've got this. You're not opening the Olympics, you're singing in front of a few guys, no biggie."

"Not to you, you have confidence radiating from you, it's as easy as breathing for you."

She smiles sadly, "Babe, you've got this. Just do it. It'll all be over in fifteen minutes."

Yeah, one way or the other.

I sigh, okay, I guess I'm up.

I stand at the side of the stage watching the band take their seats. This is it. For what it's worth. Cooper starts to make his way to the stage to take his place on the drums, a frown etched on his face, probably wondering where the heck the new singer is. I see Jen grab him and mutter something. He shakes his head, but she says something, and he gives a curt nod. Guess she's been convincing – he's not allowed on the drums right now.

I climb onto the stage and see Cooper and Jen talking near my friends. He's obviously seen Ed and Harper there and realises something is going on. I inhale deeply and breathe out slowly. Jen sees me and gives me a small nod, Cooper still hasn't seen me.

I glance at my friends who get up to stand near the stage and that's when he sees me. Every hair on my body stands on end and my heart is beating so fast, adrenaline rushing through my body.

His eyes go wide when he realises I'm standing on stage. I lean into the mic, hoping it's on. "Jen, you wanna take your place, hun?"

Cooper glances at her as though he realises. Obviously, they were talking about why Jen is going on drums. Now he gets why, although he still looks puzzled. I don't blame him.

I close my eyes and take a minute to centre myself. I can do this, I've memorised the words, if I like him as much as I say I do, which I do and more, I have to put myself out there. Show him how he's helped me and hopefully get him to like me again.

I speak into the mic. "Soooo, a little earlier than planned, I have a song I want to sing. I hope you guys don't mind."

I look directly at Cooper. "Hopefully the message I have to say will get through to the person here that I really need it to. Let's hope. Here goes."

I nod to Jen who starts the beat and then we join in. It's a song where you have to sing right from the first note, so I have to be ready.

I sing my heart out. I don't look at Cooper. I can't. I sing Liam's words about how sometimes we lose our way and want to put it behind us, and I sing as best I can. Apart from us playing, you can hear a pin drop in the room. I have everyone's attention, which, while good, is nerve-wracking. But once I start to sing, I close my eyes at points and lose myself in this beautiful song. Yes, this is scary but there is nowhere else I'd rather be than on this stage, singing or playing guitar. It's where I was born to be. I get that now. I have never felt like I belonged somewhere so much in all my life. I've found me.

The song ends and nerves creep back in because this is when I find out whether or not he will forgive me.

Quietness falls over the room until the last note has finished playing and then the crowd gathered erupts into cheers and whistles...it's amazing. There are around twenty people in this room, yet it feels like I've conquered the world as I smile shyly at them.

Finally, my eyes rest on his.

He's standing with his brother, staring at me. I take a deep breath and step away from the mic, waiting for him to make a move. I need his answer one way or the other.

Please, Coop, don't keep me hanging. Please.

He moves forward toward the stage. He strides onto it and comes to stand before me, still not saying a word.

In a flash, he puts his hand on my neck and his lips on mine. Everyone cheers again. Relief overwhelms me as I wind my hands around his neck and sink into the kiss. I tilt my head to give him better access and his lips part as his tongue brushes my lips, I open them and we deepen the kiss. There in front of everyone. Me! The shy girl. Turns out, kissing Cooper trumps shyness.

I break off after a moment and look at him, searching his eyes. "Does this mean you forgive me?"

He gives me a lopsided grin. "What do you think?"

"We have a lot to talk about, I need to explain. Meet me backstage?"

He nods and jumps off the stage to go to his brother and our friends, they're all patting him on the back and grinning, I turn to the rest of the band and give them a goofy thumbs up.

I lean in as though whispering. "It worked guys!"

"You think?" Jen asks grinning.

Jay speaks. "Heidi, you are so in the band."

I shake my head, "That's not what this was about."

"I don't care. You are in the band, you are singing our songs, one hundred per cent, Jesus, you can sing."

I blush, "Thanks," I whisper.

Ben speaks, "How can you be so shy and perform and sing like that?"

I laugh, "I have absolutely no idea."

"You have a seriously amazing voice and what a song choice."

I thank them all and go backstage, hoping Cooper and I will finally get things sorted...

Chapter Twenty-Five

♥

Heidi

I make my way backstage, which is a small area off the back of the stage where we keep all the instruments when no one is playing, so basically a storage room with a couple of seats.

Cooper walks in from around the other side at the same time that I get there.

He smiles at me. "Come here."

I walk over to him and he envelopes me in a hug. His arms around me feel so good. I'm surrounded by him. I've missed him, even though it's only been a matter of days.

"I'm sorry, Cooper," I say muffled into his shoulder.

"I'm getting that."

"Stop. I mean it. I'll never lie to you again."

He sighs and releases me, "Why did you do it in the first place?"

"Mostly because I didn't want to hurt your feelings about how my parents felt towards you when it was totally misguided. I knew you'd think badly of them and maybe think I wasn't worth the effort. You were already dealing with my anxiety thing so well, finding out about this would have been too much, you would have walked away." I take a deep breath, I need to tell him the next bit even though it's mortifying, "and well, I've liked you, for a while."

He raises his eyebrows, "Have you?"

I nod, "Yeah, and that part of me was the selfish part, I'd liked you for a while and you were paying me attention, so I wanted to let it play out, enjoy being with you."

He sighs and puts his hands on my arms, holding them gently. "Heid, I liked you too, how can you think you wouldn't be worth the hassle?"

"You *know* why, the anxiety, plus the sneaking around. Anyway, I was wrong obviously, I messed up, hence the song." I smile.

"You were amazing up there." He whispers.

We stare at each other for a while and his eyes drop to my mouth, then back to my eyes. "Are we done talking?"

I shake my head, as much as I want to kiss him, I need to know where I stand and I need to tell him about mum and dad's change of heart.

"Damn." He says, with a smirk on his face.

"My sister came to visit this week, she talked to my parents, said they'd been being unfair, that they treat me differently, and of course, because it was her talking, they listened. They said they're gonna try to be better, going to trust me more and let me behave like a sixteen-year-old girl. They also said that whatever happened with us two they are going to apologise to you and your parents for not believing you in the first place, they get that they were out of line.

He sighs, "That's good."

"Too little too late, but at least they don't mind us seeing each other...if that's what you wanted to do. If you decided, you know... that you'd forgive me..."

"Heidi?"

"Yeah?"

"Are you done talking now?"

I nod. Now it has to be his turn to speak.

I remember one thing. "Oh wait!"

He rolls his eyes, "What now?"

I swallow. "I'm falling in love with you." My heart is hammering through my chest. "Okay, your turn."

His eyes go soft and he slides his arms around my waist. "Heid, I'm well and truly falling too, if not already there."

My body sags with relief, I didn't realise I'd been holding it so tensely.

I smile at him, "Now we know where we stand."

He nods, "Yeah, we do, now are we done?"

I give a quick nod, "Absolutely."

"Then come here."

He pulls my body into him until it is full length against his. His hand cups my face as his head descends. I've missed kissing him so much. His mouth is on mine and my whole body sighs. Yes, this is what I've been missing. I open my mouth and this time the tip of my tongue runs along his lips. He groans and opens his mouth, inviting me in and we kiss and kiss. His hand at my waist goes to the waistband on my jeans and t-shirt which is cropped and his hand touches my skin there, making my whole body tingle.

I lift my hands and place them on the back of his neck, fingering his hair there. He breaks off and bites my bottom lip lightly and runs kisses all down my jawline, getting hold of my head with both hands. "You are beautiful." He murmurs as he kisses along my jaw. The words are so near my ear as he whispers them as they send shivers all through my body.

"Cooper..." is all I can manage to say as fairies have carried away my brain.

" You are amazing, you are everything, but the thing that makes you so special is you have no idea you're all those things."

His eyes are soft as he looks at me again and I slide my hand down his neck onto his chest.

"You're amazing too, Coop. You make me feel strong, like I can do anything."

He shakes his head. "You did all that, I just gave you the motivation to get past it and get on stage. You're in the band by the way."

"Yeah, I believe so."

"You okay with that?"

I nod. "Yeah, I'm a bad-ass rock chick now, didn't you know?"

"You always were, but you just needed someone to help bring it out of you."

And I realise he was right. At the end of it all, I was the one that got on that stage and sang, no one else, and I want to do it again and again because what a rush!

Pride and confidence, yes confidence, something new for me, rushes through me and I grab onto his t-shirt at the sides.

"Thought we were done talking?" I raise my eyebrows at him and he leans in to kiss me again.

We walk into the Apollo and the whole place is buzzing. The band that is going to play is one of my favourites and Coop loves them too. We are a couple now, it's been a month since I sang to him and things couldn't be better, they've been amazing in fact. He bought tickets to this band, which I'm so excited about.

I turn to him, "I still can't believe you got these tickets." He is so thoughtful.

He shrugs, "I got lucky, there was only seated left and I knew you wouldn't want to be standing in those crowds with no way to get out."

See? Thoughtful. He understands that being stuck in a crowd wouldn't help my anxiety, so he got us seats. Even more brownie points because he'd prefer to be standing there near the stage for sure.

"Thank you." I squeeze his hand.

He bends and kisses my cheek, "You are welcome."

"My boyfriend is the best." I beam at him.

"Yeah? My girlfriend is pretty awesome too."

"Not prettier than me I hope?"

He shakes his head, "No one is prettier than you."

"Oh, I feel kind of sorry for her."

He shakes his head, "Oh don't feel sorry for her, I love her."

My heart stops. Going from messing around to totally serious. We said we were both falling for each other at The Hideaway when we made up, but we've said nothing about that since. He loves me?

"Come again?"

He looks at me softly, I'm getting so addicted to that look on his face. "I love you, Heidi."

I lick my lips, my mouth suddenly dry. "I love you too."

He kisses me on the mouth, lingering a little longer than he should.

"I'm glad you gave me another chance."

His eyes darken, he doesn't like it when I talk about that, about how we weren't together. "Hey, I don't want to hear you talk about that again, okay. Both of us will mess up, no doubt it'll be my turn next, and when I do, we will sort it out. Don't beat yourself up for what you did. We only need to go forward."

I nod. "Thanks, babe."

"I love it when you call me babe."

"Do you?"

He nods, "Oh yeah, sexy as hell!"

I bat him on the arm and we settle in to watch the concert.

The first song comes on and happiness floods me. For now, I can let go of my anxiety, I'm contented. Happy. I love him and he feels the same way about me. I'm now the lead singer in a band, no gigs yet but we practice all the time. Mum and Dad have heard us play and they've met Cooper. All went well after the apology and Cooper's parents were graceful in accepting. I still can't look his dad in the eye after he caught us kissing like that, but I'm getting there.

I think back to the person I was a couple of months ago and I hardly recognise her. Living in fear does no one any good I see that now, but I didn't know how to be anything else. This new me, she kicks butt and I like her. The old Heidi will always be there, she's part of who I am but now I can enjoy life and be grateful, instead of being terrified all the time.

This Heidi looks at her boyfriend and raises the hand that she's holding, turning it around and kissing it. He leans into her and kisses her neck behind her ear. "Love you."

Oh yeah, a girl could get used to this.

Epilogue

Charlie

I walk across the school yard with Liam and Edward, the girls from the bus trailing behind. Bloody Mondays, I hate them. I hate school full stop, actually. Does anyone actually like school? Ah well, only a couple more weeks in year ten and then I'll be top of the school, one more year to go then I'm out of here. At least it's my favourite subject next. Art. I could draw all day.

Rosie, Liam's girlfriend, and Riley her best friend, are behind us, I pick up what they're saying.

I overhear Riley say, "Yeah, apparently she's gonna be on our bus from September, doesn't seem two minutes since that was you Rosie, now I feel like you've been here forever."

My ears prick up. A new girl? On our bus? I'm interested already. You see, I'm desperate for a girlfriend. I'm pretty open about it, I tell everyone. I mean, is it too much to ask? I want someone to put their arms around me and I can hold them and kiss the top of their head – now that I'm actually tall enough to do that. I want what my friends have and it's my own fault that I don't have it. Girls don't take me seriously, to them I'm one of the rugby lads, one that always jokes around, but none of them like me like that. Maybe they think that because I don't take myself seriously, that I wouldn't take them seriously either. Plus, rugby lads do have a bit of a reputation for messing girls around, but why are they including me in that? I'd be a great boyfriend!

I've noticed a little more attention from girls though recently, since I shot up and lost a bit of weight. Who wants a guy for a boyfriend that messes around all the time, likes to draw Anime and in his spare time likes to go to Comic Cons and is obsessed with Marvel?

Talk about geek central. How do I find someone that would get me, with my interests? I can't exactly chat up girls at Comic Cons. No actually, believe me, I've tried.

Life's crap at the minute. I hate school, my parents are recently divorced and all the fun that comes with that. And to top it all off, Dad has started dating again, which I hate. How long is it since the divorce was finalised, about an hour? Maybe I'm overexaggerating but it is only a matter of weeks ago. Bloody Dad has a new one tonight. He wants me to meet her at dinner, but no way. London Comic Con tickets go on sale tonight, so I'll be in my room ready.

So due to my life being a mess, I feel the need to have a laugh where I can. I mess around and act daft, tell jokes and even make jokes at the girl's expense, yeah, bad right? I can't bloody help it, my mouth runs away with me!

I love rugby though, a chance to barge through a load of people with a ball and call it sport, it's a great way to destress.

I need more info, I turn to Riley, "What's this? We're getting a new girl?"

She nods, "Yeah apparently. We're losing Ed and Cooper now that Coop can drive, they're deserting us, so there's space, and a girl is starting in the sixth form in September."

I nod, "Ooh, what do we know? Come on girls tell all. Does she love geeky guys that are into Marvel but also cool as hell cos they play rugby?"

"Well, who wouldn't?" Rosie jokes

"Right?" I say affronted. "Seriously, what do we know?"

Riley shakes her head, "Nothing, I'm sorry, the bus driver mentioned it this morning, that is the extent of my knowledge."

"Well, you're no use, are you? This could be the girl of my dreams we're talking about."

She shrugs, "Sorry, you're gonna have to wait until September."

Hmmm, that's like eight weeks away, I'm sure I could do that.

*****

You will get Charlie's story in the next book (Book 5) of Arrowsmith High...

If you want to keep up to date on any coming releases, beta reader offers, or other things, then please sign up to my newsletter here.

Thank you so much for reading my novel. I hope you enjoyed it! The best way to thank an author for writing a great book is to leave an honest review. I would be so grateful if you did that.

If you want to connect with me:

Facebook: https://www.facebook.com/MJ-Ray-Author-106849384519134

Amazon Author Page: https://www.amazon.com/MJ-Ray/e/B08LDWNL9W/ref=dp_byline_cont_pop_ebooks_1

authormjray@outlook.com

Bookbub: MJ Ray Books - BookBub

Manufactured by Amazon.ca
Acheson, AB